DR. DONG'S C

"Fifteen years ago I was stricken—and I do mean stricken—with arthritis. It was so bad I couldn't swim and I even hated to walk . . . The pain was so intense aspirin offered practically no relief. I was an exceedingly active woman and suddenly arthritis threatened not only to cripple me but my whole approach to living.

"I went to Dr. Dong and he put me on the diet. At first I was appalled. How on earth would I survive? What would I feed dinner guests? What could I eat when I went out to dinner?

"Three weeks after I started the diet the pain and the crippling disappeared . . ."

AND TODAY, FIFTEEN YEARS LATER, JANE BANKS IS STILL ON THE DIET, A HAPPY WOMAN AND CO-AUTHOR OF THIS BESTSELLING BOOK.

THE ARTHRITIC'S COOKBOOK

The Arthritic's Cookbook

COLLIN H. DONG, M.D.
and
JANE BANKS

BANTAM BOOKS
TORONTO · NEW YORK · LONDON · SYDNEY

THE ARTHRITIC'S COOKBOOK

*A Bantam Book / published by arrangement with
Thomas Y. Crowell Company*

PRINTING HISTORY

Thomas Y. Crowell edition published August 1973
2nd printing ...... August 1973   4th printing .. September 1973
3rd printing .. September 1973   5th printing ...... October 1973
6th printing .... November 1973
A selection of the Cook Book Guild August 1974
A condensation appeared in WOMAN'S DAY *August 1973*

Bantam edition / January 1975
2nd printing ...... August 1977   4th printing .... February 1979
3rd printing .... August 1978   5th printing .. December 1979
6th printing .... December 1980

to JEROME TAYLOR

Contents

Introduction

ARTHRITIS IS a malady that conjures up in our mind's eye a picture of a crotchety old man sitting in a wheel chair; his every movement is painful and awkward. Invariably he holds a pair of crutches or a cane in his knobby, clawlike hands to aid him in making short trips from his home base, the wheelchair.

At the age of thirty-five, after practicing medicine for seven years, I was afflicted with this baffling disease. For three years, the only relief from the agony of this disorder was taking large doses of aspirin and other related analgesics ordered by my doctors.

After consulting and being treated by many specialists, locally and elsewhere, my arthritis became progressively worse. In addition to the wracking pains in my various joints, I developed a generalized dermatitis. My last consultant, like all the others, was in a quandary. He told me that there was nothing he could suggest for further treatment of these two diseases, my arthritis and my skin problem. His final advice was to see a psychiatrist.

I knew that I was slowly going crazy, but I

1

wanted to think that I was not yet ready for a head shrinker. Needless to say, after the last pronouncement I had a soul-searching and sleepless night. But it also happened to be a fateful one, for when I looked into the mirror the next morning, I saw an appalling, repulsive reflection. That image shocked me into a new consciousness—not unlike an electric-shock treatment by a psychiatrist. The man in this reflected image had lost most of his black curly hair and was almost bald. The smooth yellow skin of his face was inflamed, swollen, cracked and caked with a weeping exudate. His eyebrows were scanty, and his slanty eyelids were puffy and showed only a small slit of the eyes. He could barely lift his hands to wash his face due to the excruciating pain and stiffness in his shoulders. This was me! A physician who had been trained in modern medicine and who had been under the medical care of his most prominent colleagues.

During the three years of this illness I had read all the scientific papers, books, and journals dealing with the treatment of arthritis and its related diseases. The medical world up to that moment had not found the cause of arthritis and had no cure for this problem. Every rheumatologist whom I had consulted gave the same treatment that was outlined in the medical books and journals, and I had passively accepted their advice and therapy. Now they had given up my case. I was on my own. I was faced with the problem of finding some means of therapy to alleviate this ailment if I was not to be assigned to one of those wheelchairs for the rest of my life.

My traditional education and indoctrination had conditioned my mind to accept without question the teachings of the famous physicians I consulted. Now I was confronted with an emergency —a sink-or-swim situation. I had heard stories of a drowning man grasping at straws and how his whole life history flashed through his mind an instant before unconsciousness. Although I was not drowning, something similar happened to me. I also had a flashback with an instant recall of my past life.

What I remembered most vividly at that moment was my father saying to me, as he said to all his nine children whenever any of us became ill: *Bing chung how yup, woh chung how chut.* Literally translated this means, "Sickness enters through the mouth, and catastrophe comes out of the mouth."

I had forgotten this sage folk observation in my pursuit of Western higher education and scientific knowledge. Now that all the expertise had failed me, I was grasping at straws. Incredible as it may sound, this axiom was the straw that eventually rescued me from a wheelchair. This old adage pointed me in another direction. Perhaps I had been putting some "sickness" through my mouth for a long time without realizing it.

For up to this very moment, I had given very little consideration to the problem of nutrition and its effect on the human body, except that I knew I had to eat to live and work. Throughout my life I had been on a more or less simple Chinese diet consisting mainly of beef, pork, chicken, fish, vegetables, and rice. When I started the practice of medicine in 1931, I gradually changed to a diet like that of most affluent Americans. The reason for this transition has been suggested by Dr. S. I. Hayakawa, the famous semanticist, in his great book *Symbol, Status, and Personality:* "Advertising spends untold millions to build up connotations, to teach us to put implicit faith in the affective overtones with which 'brand names' are invested. . . . Advertising, as currently practiced, is almost entirely a matter of pound, pound, pounding into people word-mindedness to the exclusion of fact-mindedness."

Being a busy practitioner, this subliminal propaganda produced by the dream-factories of Madison Avenue compelled me to eat brand A orange juice and fruit; brand B milk and ice cream; brand C bacon, eggs, beef, pork, chicken, and lamb; brand D vegetables, green and yellow; brand E bread and cereals.

How can such a wonderfully balanced diet make anyone sick? Every book on diet and nutrition written by famous doctors, dietitians, or nutritionists recommends just such a diet. Yet I was crippled with two chronic diseases that defied the attempts of the scientific medical practitioners to cure. Little did I know that I was also afflicted with a third disease, "word-mindedness."

Generally in a crisis the instincts come to the rescue. It happened here too—"fact-mindedness" suddenly entered my confused mentality. I started questioning the validity of the advice and writings of brand-name authorities. After all, I was descended from a culture that was 6,000 years old and from people who had never had any brand-name foods.

Their daily sustenance for thousands of years has been the basic ingredients that nature gave to all the people of the universe—meat, vegetables, rice, or wheat.

The past history of my immediate family, nine

brothers and sisters and my parents, had always manifested a high degree of allergy to foods: father to pork; Dr. Eugene to wheat and milk; Ella and Alice to turkey and melon; Dr. Hubert to eggs; Harriet to seafood; Lily to green leafy vegetables; Dr. Emma to tomatoes and milk; and Dr. Marion to seafood and oranges. Mother, with her peaches-and-cream complexion, was not allergic to anything. However, I, Collin, the glutton of the family, was allergic to milk, wheat, eggs, and fruit —especially oranges.

Allergy to food has been chronicled in Chinese medical literature for many centuries. The aphorism "Sickness enters through the mouth and catastrophe comes out of the mouth" was no doubt originally propagated by the first emperor of China, Shen Nung. He ordered pregnant women to stop eating shellfish because it caused *fung non,* which we call hives or urticaria. He reasoned that if shellfish can cause poisoning of the skin, it could cause ill effects on the unborn child. Horse meat was another forbidden food, because it was thought that it caused miscarriages.

With these salient facts in mind—the dictum of Emperor Shen Nung, the past history of my family, and the arthritis that had baffled the doctors—I launched myself on what we would call a "poor man's diet," comprising simple meat, vegetables, and rice. I also continued to use a variety of medications and ointments to ease my symptoms.

At first the experimental efforts were not rewarding, but gradually, by eliminating certain medications, especially aspirin, and different food components in my diet, I began feeling a general improvement. I discovered that there and then the most satisfactory diet for my arthritis was a combination of seafood, vegetables, and rice.

To my utter amazement, in a few short weeks there was a metamorphosis. I was able to sleep again, for the fitful nightmares of years were gone. I was able to shave again, for the skin became soft and pliable and did not "weep." I was agile again, for I went from 195 pounds to 150 pounds. I was able to play golf again, for the stiffness and pain in my joints disappeared. I was able to smile again, for the psychological torture of years was alleviated. I had almost a complete remission from my crippling disease.

This remission has miraculously lasted for thirty-one years. On my next birthday I shall be seventy years of age. Every morning I play either nine or eighteen holes of golf, or I practice hitting four to five hundred golf balls and I pick them up myself. My golf score will vary from the high seventies to the low eighties, depending upon how much I am betting with Charlie Lazzari.

Every three to six months I take a blood test. Last week the Multi-Panel test was within normal limits. My electrocardiograph was normal. The gastrointestinal series indicated that I had a healed duodenal ulcer. No doubt it had been incurred during my illness more than thirty years ago.

Today my life-style and daily routine, in addition to my golf, consists of making morning rounds at the hospital and answering the complaints of tenants in two apartment houses, one of seventy-two units and the other of thirty-one units. In the afternoon I treat from thirty to forty patients five days a week. After office hours I make occasional house calls if necessary, or attend corporation and hospital staff meetings.

My present diet is now restricted to fish, vegetables, and rice. I sleep soundly for about five to six hours every night. My one indulgence in life is that I have a chauffeur to drive me to and from work, and house calls. The driver is my beautiful, patient, and talented wife. Her remuneration is an annual adventurous vacation to faraway places around the globe.

My dramatic recovery convinced me that one of the causes of rheumatic diseases is allergy to food and additives. Upon returning to my medical practice, I incorporated a diet in addition to the usual chemical therapy for all my patients. I give them a lecture on the subject of nutrition in relation to health and illness. I warn them against the hazards of eating processed and prepared foods containing artificial flavoring, coloring, chemical preservatives, and other additives. The rewards of these few minutes of conversation with the patient are immeasurable in getting their cooperation and confidence.

In the past thirty years I have treated thousands of cases of rheumatic diseases. The high percentage of remissions from pain and misery with my method is remarkable. I have been asked by my many patients why I did not disseminate my knowledge to help others. Why was a book not written?

The answer is a simple one. I did not have the courage to fight the medical establishment. We live in a world where it takes many years to build one's professional reputation. My method of treatment is an empirical one. It was not established on a scientific or theoretical basis accepted by the medical world.

As an example of what has to be disproved and disputed, let me quote a booklet I was given when I recently attended an eight-hour seminar on rheumatic diseases. The pamphlet is titled *The Truth About Diet and Arthritis*, and is issued by the Arthritis Foundation. Its first statement is: "There is no special diet for arthritis. No specific food has anything to do with causing it. And no specific diet will cure it." Further on, the pamphlet states: "The fact is, the possibility that some dietary factor either causes or can help control arthritis has been thoroughly and scientifically investigated and disproved. The only exceptions are in gout." These authoritative, arbitrary, and tyrannical words were issued on an expensive, beautifully printed, brown, blue, and white paper by the Arthritis Foundation.

I would have accepted the validity and word-mindedness of these promulgations without question if, in the first place, the remission of my arthritic affliction had not lasted more than thirty years, and, secondly, if my painful symptoms had not recurred whenever I deviated from my diet— and, finally, if the thousands of patients with arthritis that I have treated over the years had not had such dramatic relief from their pain and suffering.

Furthermore, another piece of literature issued by the Arthritis Foundation, *Diet and Arthritis—A Handbook for Patients*, states:

But there is overwhelming evidence that nutritionally balanced meals eaten regularly benefit anyone's overall health, muscle tone, and in the case of arthritis, build ability to resist the wear and tear of the disease . . . in general the good diet for anyone, whether you have arthritis or not, is based on a selection from four food groups. Briefly, they are the milk group, the meat group, the vegetable and fruit group, and the bread and cereal group.

In other words arthritic sufferers should eat anything and everything they find in the local food markets and plenty of it. Yet there is overwhelming evidence that serious illnesses and even catastrophe result from eating certain food components. As I am writing this, my wife puts in my hands a copy of the *San Francisco Examiner*, dated June 7, 1972, in which Dr. Jean Mayer, professor of nutrition at Harvard University, writes: "Ten-year-old Michael Gryzybinski died. That's right, died—from an anaphylactic reaction due to ingested peanuts." This death was due to angioedema of the larynx, or, in common terms, asphyxiation due to the swelling of the throat caused by an allergic reaction after eating peanuts.

The American Academy of Allergy constantly issues information about and case histories of serious diseases caused by allergy. It is estimated that more than 100 million Americans are suffering from some form of allergic disease, and perhaps one-quarter of them are seriously ill without being correctly diagnosed and treated. Moreover, in the study of allergies it has been found that any item of food mentioned in the four recommended groups by the Arthritis Foundation can be allergens, the substances that cause the allergies.

The most common category of nutritional components for Americans is the milk group. But there is such a thing as milk intolerance, increasingly understood by the scientists. Practically every recipe in the American diet contains small or large amounts of milk or milk powder. However, Theodore Bayless, M.D., of the Johns Hopkins University School of Medicine, says: "Among white adults of Scandinavian or Western European extraction only 2 to 8 percent are lactose intolerant . . . in sharp contrast to the 60 to 80 percent prevalence in samples of Greek Cypriots, Arabs and Ashkenazi Jews, 70 percent among American Negroes."

This means that many millions of Americans are allergic to milk. In the light of this report, the recommendation of milk or milk products to arthritics could hinder or complicate the recovery from this disease.

The impact of rheumatic diseases on the American economy is shown in the report of the *Geriatric Times* News Service for March 1969:

America's battle against the arthritic and rheumatic diseases is a frustrating campaign that now involves more than 150 federally-funded research projects and which costs individuals and the nation more than $3.6 billion every year in various social and economic implications.

No other disorders cause more prolonged misery to a greater number of people in the United States than do these diseases. The three most crippling forms of arthritis (rheumatoid arthritis, gout, and osteoarthritis) cause unemployment each year to the equivalent of nearly half a million people, cost the government nearly $200 million annually in lost income taxes, and account for about 12 percent of all welfare expenditures through subsistence allowances to arthritics unable to support themselves. No price tags, however, can be placed on the untold suffering, pain, invalidism, and mental anguish which these disorders impose on individuals and their families. About 17 million people in the United States afflicted with arthritis look to research for a means to relieve their suffering.

Confronted with such a dismal report, I think now is the time for research organizations and foundations to reappraise their concepts and encourage investigation in every direction. Dr. Charles L. Christian of Columbia Presbyterian Medical Center, New York City, says: "With our current limited knowledge of this disease, we cannot completely ignore any lead—no matter how inconsequential it may seem at first." And may I add, even in the direction of dietary factors as a possible cause of arthritis.

During the past few years there have been remarkable changes in the attitudes of the medical establishment. Long-haired interns have had strikes against hospital authorities. Bearded young doctors have interrupted the usual staid, formal meetings of the American Medical Association. Activists within every local medical society are attempting to break the ties of local and state branches with the national association.

Only a few weeks ago the San Francisco Medical Society had a "happening," an unheard-of event. It allowed two unlicensed Chinese acupuncturists to enter its hallowed halls to demonstrate on three patients in the auditorium. One of the patients was the president-elect of the California Medical Association. As I sat in the audience, the success or failure of the acupuncture demonstration was not the uppermost thought in my mind; I was fascinated by the fact that the Medical Society would allow such an innovation.

These episodes gave me the determination to voice my opinion on the subject of my own method of treating arthritis.

Such emphatic statements as the one quoted earlier—"The fact is, the possibility that some dietary factor either causes or can help control arthritis has been thoroughly and scientifically investigated and disproved"—are not only unwarranted but discourage further research.

Let me ask, Who were the people who did all this research? What is their background? Are they just doctors, nutritionists, and dietitians sitting in a weekly conference, smoking their cigarettes and stuffing themselves with breakfasts, luncheons, and dinners served to them contaminated with preservatives, artificial flavoring and coloring, and monosodium glutamate?

If any of these research groups wish to investigate the nutritional aspect of the etiology of arthritis, let me make a suggestion! Ask for volunteers among the group of dedicated rheumatologists who are willing to spend a few months of their lives to go into food-processing factories and the kitchens of restaurants, hotels, convalescent homes, and sandwich makers to see how the food is prepared and what chemicals are added to preserve it, color it, or make it taste better for the consumer. Then if they wish to investigate further, they should go into the slaughterhouses and watch how the meats are prepared and what is done with the leftovers and the various organs of the animals, which eventually become hot dogs, luncheon meats, and sausages. Then, and only then, can they say, "Dietary factors have been thoroughly investigated." And if among the investigating team there should be one who is afflicted with arthritis, his opinion will bear more weight.

At this juncture, let me warn my readers that diet alone will not cure arthritis or any other disease. I do not rule out medication. But medication alone will not cure diseases either. What I am suggesting is a radically modified diet supplemented by whatever moderate medication may be necessary in the individual case. And in evaluating diet, one must not forget than an affluent society consumes many highly advertised foods, food components, and preservatives, any of which can be allergenic. Eliminating these possible allergens should benefit everybody, especially the sick.

The fish diet that I recommend to my arthritic patients has been clinically shown to be effective in combination with medication. The bulletin issued by the U.S. Department of the Interior, September 1961, supports its value as a substitute for the usual beef, lamb, and pork proteins in any diet. This bulletin states:

Fish can be consumed three times daily due to its nutritional values, and in general is applicable to any diets designed to yield (1) needed biologically valuable trace minerals, (2) high levels of vitamins, especially those of the B complex system, (3) reduction of sodium intake and consequent reduction in body water retention, (4) reduction in hard fat intake and restoration of fatty acid balance between hard and soft fats, (5) high levels of readily available biologically complete, easily digestible proteins, and (6) increase in body energy food intake with maximum ease of metabolic utilization.

The following scientific evidence is in support of my hypothesis that arthritis is an allergic disease: (1) As early as 1967 Dr. Robert Good of the University of Minneapolis Medical School found that ". . . in patients who are unable to make gamma globulin and antibodies, arthritis is thirty times more common than it is in the general population." (2) Recently Dr. David Mumford of the Baylor College of Medicine, Houston, Texas, stated: "New information about the two-part immune system has opened up the study of immunoglobulin, large blood cells that are prototype antibodies. So far, we know about five of these. If one is lacking, for instance, it may lead to severe allergies. If another is not present, the body may have no defense against a whole variety of infectious diseases."

The interpretation of these two scientific gems, which are emphatically in support of my concept, is that arthritis patients lack the ability to produce immunoglobulin or antibodies to protect themselves against allergens which cause the arthritis. I have found that my dietary regimen with medication, the objective of which is to eliminate the allergens, is clinically effective in the treatment of arthritis.

However, before anyone considers himself an arthritic, the disease should be diagnosed by a competent physician. Then, with his aid and direction, I am sure that you will benefit by changing your own confused nutritional pattern to one that is logical and practical.

In conclusion, I am writing this introduction in the hope that the legitimate field of American medicine will see the way clear to add one more weapon to its armamentarium to battle against the ravages of arthritis. The weapon is my father's slogan:

BING CHUNG HOW YUP, WOH CHUNG
HOW CHUT.

—Collin H. Dong, M.D.
San Francisco
June 1972

1

It Works for Me

I WAS ONE of the 40 million arthritics in the United States. In fact, I was fast becoming one of the 13 million disabled or crippled arthritics in the United States. I came by it naturally, as the saying goes: There is a familial history of arthritis and related diseases, such as gout. (Gout is rare in women, although I have it.) I had a severely crippled brother who died from the effects of a medication for rheumatoid arthritis, so I was understandably wary of the drugs being prescribed by the numerous doctors I progressed through in my search for help.

I was born a crazy optimist; I felt sure that somewhere there was another answer to my problem, something more reasonable than fifteen aspirin a day plus the gamble of the cortisone-derivative drugs. The answer came, as it so often does, through a friend. Observing my stiff, painful movements and my swollen, knotty hands, he said, "Jane, we had a man in our plant who was cured of arthritis."

"Cured?" I said. "But that's impossible!"

"Perhaps it's not a cure in the strictest sense," my friend explained, "but six months ago he was very nearly unable to work. He's an upholsterer, and his hands were so stiff he couldn't use them. Today he's fine, perfectly normal. He's been under treatment by Dr. Dong, a Chinese doctor."

Remember, I was in sad shape. I was unable to open my hands completely, I had a persistent pain in one hip, and the large joint of one foot was at times too painful for a shoe. We had recently bought a house on a beautiful lagoon because I love to swim; the pain in my shoulders made swimming impossible. Is it any wonder I literally leapt at my friend's suggestion?

Through him I received an appointment with the doctor. His office, with its Chinese decor, seemed quite foreign; I found him very charming. He was lean and fit with quick, precise movements; he looked about forty-five, but I learned later he is almost seventy.

"Tell me everything you eat in a day," was his first demand. I outlined what I considered an extremely healthy high-protein, low-calorie diet consisting mainly of meat, eggs, and cheese.

"No wonder," he said, shaking his head. "From now on you will eat only fish and vegetables. Later we'll add an occasional breast of chicken. That is," he added, "if you want to stay well."

"But," I asked, "does such a simple, restricted diet give you all the nutrients you need?"

"Let me explain it this way. The basis of foods is meat, vegetables, and starch. The amount consumed depends on the individual; actually he should be eating only to replace the breaking-down process of the body. He needs protein, vegetables, and carbohydrates—the protein to replace cells, the vegetables for minerals and vitamins. A diet restricted to these elements will slow down the aging process in addition to increasing the life span. Incidentally," he added, "life is a paradox. When we are young and can tolerate the rich foods, most of us cannot afford Trader Vic's and 21; when you can afford them your body no longer can handle the fats and spices."

"Is that why so many people have arthritis?"

"Naturally an unwise diet will have varying adverse effects. However, arthritis and its related diseases are all too often the result." He went on to explain that most people lose about ten pounds in the first week of the treatment, due to the high-protein, low-calorie characteristic of the diet. "Vegetables and oils have a most beneficial effect on skin tone," he added. "However, additives, preservatives, and spices are not necessary to body functioning."

For the first time in many months I began to feel hopeful. However, I love to eat, and love to cook. I felt somewhat dismayed at what I considered a dreary culinary prospect. "Isn't it awfully boring?" I asked.

"Not at all. With a little ingenuity you can make it a gourmet affair. Using the basic acceptable ingredients, plus vegetable oils and margarine, you'll find you can come up with some highly satisfying and tempting dishes. You'll have rice, of course, but go easy on refined white flour, whole grains, and cereals. You'll learn to be a careful label reader and find the brands of things that are acceptable. For instance, I recently discovered a delicious natural wheat bread containing no additives or preservatives. There are more and more natural foods available, thanks to the young."

"You make it all sound so simple," I said. "It's almost too good to be true!"

Two weeks later I was almost completely free of pain, and now, after four years, I find it hard to remember exactly what it was like. The swelling disappeared gradually, and the stiffness with it. It seems to me I simply woke up one morning and realized I wasn't stiff anymore. I feel absolutely marvelous now, and lead a completely normal life again. What is normal for me is a little more active than for the average woman my age; in addition to having a career—interior design—and a heavy schedule of entertaining, I do all the housework and take care of a rather extensive and demanding garden. I have a long swim every day, in season, and on weekends my husband and I take long rides on our racing bicycles. I have twice as much energy as I did ten years ago, and one by one my friends are capitulating to my diet just because I *look* so much better than I did ten years ago. I'm thin, my hair is shiny, and my skin has a good healthy color; I'm more than happy about it all and totally committed to a lifetime of eating to stay that way. (An incidental note might be added here; on my last visit to the dentist to have my teeth cleaned I was a source of immense interest to the technician. Everyone's gums bleed when being scraped and prodded, but the technician called in the dentist to tell him she had never seen such tough gums, such nonbleeders. When I suggested that my diet might have something to do with it, my dentist nodded happily and agreed that this was undoubtedly the case.)

However, I do not claim this diet will *cure* you; obviously such claims can be made only after long research and documentation. I do know the diet worked for me, and for many, many other people, and if your symptoms are alleviated it will make me very happy.

I'm no medical expert, but I believe one of the reasons this works is because the body is getting what nature intended it to have in the first place. Sound, proper nutrition means furnishing the body with all the vitamins and minerals it needs; proper nutrition should also mean that the body is protected from poisons.

The fact that there are 40 million arthritics in the United States, according to the Arthritis Foundation, certainly has something to do with the increasingly deteriorating diet of the past few generations: an increase in foods from which all the value has been processed, foods treated with preservatives and additives that in some cases have proven to be extremely dangerous.

All arthritic patients are by now well aware of the hard fact that there is as yet no positive cure for arthritis. However, medical research has made strides in proving that the human life span could be expanded twenty to forty years by limiting the intake of starch, sugar, dairy products, and meat. Long-term studies of diet and aging have shown that the person who cuts his calorie intake 60 percent by avoiding the above-listed foods is more resistant to disease and has a longer, more vigorous life. Also there is evidence that eliminating white refined flour and sugar has had a therapeutic effect on many arthritics. Incidentally, Sam, our Labrador retriever, had developed arthritis in his hip. I took him off his huge daily ration of cooked meat and started giving him only kibbled grain, plus leftover fish and vegetables with ¼ cup of corn oil. His limp disappeared almost immediately; shortly thereafter I discovered a high-protein grain product that enabled me to cut down on his calories, and now we have a lean, healthy, shiny dog again. It's the same story as with humans; as a young dog he could tolerate the diet, but as age changed his body it became necessary to make adjustments.

By now my enthusiasm for and faith in this regime must be apparent to you. Very recently I experienced a reaffirmation of this faith and enthusiasm as a result of a trip I took to the Far East. This book was completed, my husband was going to be away on a business trip, and since I had never been to the Orient, I decided the moment had come. I went to Hong Kong, Bangkok, and Singapore, and in each place found something to further strengthen my belief in this basically Oriental diet.

Although the pursuit of beauty and culture was the aim of the trip, I somehow found it to be a "people trip." The Chinese, thought-provoking as they are, certainly demonstrate the efficacy of their diet. However, I found the latter most dramatically demonstrated in Thailand. The people are most beautiful and seem to radiate good health and friendly spirit. Making the boat trips along the *klongs*, one wonders how these extremely improverished people can be so healthy— that is, until one remembers that they live on fish and their fertile soil produces vegetables in great abundance. This extends, of course, to the luxury hotels; I've never seen a seafood bar like the one in the Siam Intercontinental! Live seafood cooked to order and to perfection. And in Singapore the whole thing was more or less underlined for me by a most impressive Chinese lady with whom I had a memorable long lunch. When I commented on her choice of a beautifully poached whole fish for our entree, she said, "But of course! We Chinese have always lived this way! We know we are what we put in our bodies, and we know our bodies change daily."

Let me emphasize again that this book does not purport to be a cure for arthritis! Just about everyone has arthritis at some time or another; all this book purports to tell you is how to live.

EXERCISE

We all know that the body needs exercise in order to function properly. A moderate amount of sensible exercise will also help you to utilize these valuable foods; the improved circulation will aid in ridding your body of poisons.

I think it's safe to say that *everyone* has the basic exercise of walking available to him. No matter where or how you live, you can somehow get out and walk. The distance and pace depends on you and your condition; the important thing is to make it part of your daily routine, no matter how much you'd rather do something sedentary when you have the time. Swimming is probably considered to be the best exercise there is for any sort of arthritis. The body, being suspended in the water, is relieved of pressures and jolts, and yet the joints are being exercised. By all means take advantage of every opportunity to swim—even if it means going to a city pool in winter. (Actually, the indoor heated pools in all big cities are better for you than chilly outdoor swimming.)

My favorite exercise, both for conditioning and pleasure, is bicycling. This is a sport that's gained tremendous popularity in recent years—ten years ago, when I took to riding on the streets of San Francisco, my teen-age daughter was mortified; now everyone is doing it. Some lucky communities have installed bike paths, but in almost all places there are parks and country roads to ride on. It takes no skill—we all learned as children, and bicycling is one of those things one never forgets.

Gardening can be good exercise, too, if you don't have to crouch or kneel in one position too long, particularly on the damp ground.

2

It Worked for Them

GLADYS H., a postal employee in her thirties, had been to five doctors for treatment of clinically diagnosed rheumatoid arthritis. She was able to pass the physical tests required for her job but was in such severe pain that she found it impossible to function properly at work. As she says, she looked about ninety years old, and could hardly hold a piece of toast in her hand. At one point she spent a week in a hospital, and finally gave up on all levels, both physical and mental. She was in the depths when she happened to hear of a friend who had been treated by diet, successfully, and subsequently she made an appointment with the doctor her friend had consulted. It took her three painful hours to dress for the appointment, but her improvement was immediate and now ten months later she is well and happy. She has absolutely no pain except on those rash occasions when she lapses from the diet.

WALTER S., an insurance broker of fifty-one, felt that his life was almost over. He could barely roll out of bed in the morning, and was so exhausted after a few hours at the office that he would go home. He was in constant pain—arthritis calcium in his back, which showed in X rays, bursitis in both shoulders, a tennis elbow. An active, athletic man, he was most depressed when he had to hang up his golf clubs. He was overweight and couldn't seem to find a diet that worked. He was free of pain after a few weeks of the arthritis diet, and had lost thirty-two pounds after two months. He feels fifteen years younger. He is no longer tired, feels agile and energetic and full of well-being.

MARGARET R. watched her elderly mother becoming moribund before her eyes. Bedridden because of arthritic pain and stiffness, barely able to move, her health declined to an almost hopeless level. After one visit to the doctor and a week's adherence to the diet, she was well enough to get up. Now, after a year, she is still well and active, living a full, interesting, useful life.

JACK B., sixty-three, a construction worker, suffered from rheumatoid arthritis. He had constant pain in practically every part of his body. He went from doctor to doctor and finally, in despair, he had to stop working. At this point he saw Dr. Dong, and after only two months of the regime was able to go back to work.

RUTH H., seventy-three, hobbled into the office on a cane. Osteoarthritis affected her knees, hands, and ankles severely. She weighed 170 pounds and took 80 grains of aspirin daily. The aspirin was stopped, and a stringent diet prescribed, namely the fish and vegetable diet but excepting such items as rice, bread, and potatoes. Within one month she weighed 145 pounds, soon thereafter threw away her cane, and about a year later was married.

AUGUSTINA M., sixty-three, was crippled by osteoarthritis of the neck bones and the knees. She also suffered from migraine headaches. Since she found herself unable to leave her house, of course she was unable to work. After three months of adherence to the diet she was practically pain-free and able to return to her work and normal life.

CECILE B., sixty-nine, had generalized arthritis but suffered most acutely in the toes, acutely enough so that it was necessary to use a cane. In addition she suffered from diverticulitis and diarrhea. These latter symptoms disappeared almost immediately upon adherence to the diet; after a few months the pain from the arthritis was gone, she was able to live a normal life, and is now busy writing a book.

MARK M., three and a half, developed rheumatoid arthritis at eleven months. He was treated at the hospital, mainly with aspirin, and since the pain was mainly centered in his knees, was put in leg braces. He was carried into Dr. Dong's office. The aspirin was stopped, he was taken off milk, and after one and a half months of the regime he could walk.

JESSIE K., sixty-two, came in a much-over-weight 200 pounds. She had painful arthritis in both her knees and ankles. She was placed on the diet, and six months later, at 144 pounds, was free of pain.

LOUISE C., seventy, an active horsewoman, had such arthritic pain in the lumbar spine that she was unable to ride or, in fact, to turn over in bed. After five months on the diet she was again able to ride her horse and was pain-free.

LYDIA G., eighty, arrived in a wheelchair. She was in most severe pain day and night, especially in her knees but also in her left hip. She weighed 174 pounds, but after several months of the treatment she was down to 150 and was walking into the office.

3

The Working Elements

IN THE COMPLICATED MACHINERY of your body are all sorts of checks and balances. Vitamins and minerals are vitally important to you; all are present in the many vegetables you'll be eating. In most cases it is not necessary to add supplemental vitamins and minerals, but if you feel you need them, consult your doctor.

Actually, the primary concept of this regime is to consume only the basic, necessary foods instead of loading the body with extras it can't handle. The American public is simply eating too much!

Protein is, of course, the first thing to be considered when choosing your foods. It is universally agreed that it's of utmost importance to maintenance of the body, formation of new tissues and cells, and resistance to disease. Since arthritis is a degenerative disease, I though it wise to materially increase my daily intake of protein.

Seafood is a complete protein, completely digestible, and supplies in addition those valuable elements from the sea not available elsewhere. Of course, fresh fish is not possible for many because of geographical location, but there's always frozen fish and shellfish. Please, just read the label to be sure nothing has been added in the processing.

Of the vegetables, potatoes, cabbage, green peppers, and all the leafy greens are rich in the vitamins and minerals valuable to the arthritic. Brussels sprouts, beets, peas, beans, carrots, and celery are all very good. Make salads with raw vegetables as well as lettuce, since cooking cancels out their enzymes; serve them with shrimp, crab, or tuna and you have a complete lunch.

Sufferers from gout, a disease related to arthritis, must find out which of the vegetables listed on page 35 are to be avoided. Here common sense must enter in; everyone's body is different, and one must discover one's own anathemas by experimentation. For instance, some people might be allergic to nuts, but not all kinds of nuts. By the same token, some might be allergic to certain kinds of honey, depending on the flower from which the bee fed.

Unless you have 20-20 pluperfect vision, take your glasses with you to the grocery store. The law says that the ingredients must be listed on the label, but the size of the print is apparently not regimented. Try to buy products that have the purest ingredients; I cannot emphasize enough the importance of being a label reader. It is vital to avoid all additives and preservatives; one of your worst enemies is the chemical monosodium glutamate. The smallest amount of it can bring me days of discomfort.

Find a corn-oil margarine that is free of milk solids, and for salads mix corn oil with olive oil for flavor. There is a product called Saffola mayonnaise which is acceptable, and I should imagine available upon request. (Easterners should try health-food stores or the health-food departments of supermarkets for Balanaise or other acceptable types of safflower oil mayonnaise). I use both margarine and oil in cooking, and in very generous quantities; there is evidence that the presence of polyunsaturated fat is a factor in the strengthening of new cell membranes.

Dr. Hugh M. Sinclair of the Department of Nutrition at Oxford University, vice-president of Oxford's Magdalen College and one of the world's foremost authorities on nutrition, has discovered some interesting facts. His discoveries, based on research, indicate that many of the so-called diseases of modern civilization are apparently the end result of a strange food deficiency. The missing substances are vitamin-like compounds known as essential unsaturated fatty acids, or UFA, found primarily in corn, peanut, cottonseed, and other vegetable oils. He indicates that a UFA deficiency seems to underlie certain conditions such as arthritis, allergy, bronchial asthma, skin diseases, and ulcerative colitis, as well as heart disease. The UFA chemicals, which seem to work somewhat like vitamins, include one potent substance known chemically as linoleic acid and an even more potent compound called arachidonic acid. These chemicals, found in natural vegetable oils, are extremely sensitive to oxidation and are destroyed in the bleaching of flour, the frying of foods, and the hardening of natural oils that occurs in the manufacture of margarine.

If you inspect the label on the bottle of safflower oil, you will discover an interesting table of ratios between polyunsaturated and saturated fats. Safflower oil has a ratio of 9 to 1, corn oil 5.3 to 1, soybean oil 3.9 to 1, and cottonseed oil 2 to 1. Obviously these figures on the label, derived from a 1959 report of the U.S. Department of Agriculture, should not be ignored.

Whenever I find myself in the kitchen with a little time on my hands, I make a supply of frequently used items. Onions, garlic, and parsley are invaluable in this sort of cookery, and I chop onions and parsley and store them in jars with tight tops in the refrigerator. All my old chunks of leftover French bread go in the blender for bread crumbs and are also stored in a jar.

Other acceptable seasonings, in addition to the parsley and onions just mentioned, are garlic, bay leaf, salt, and soy sauce. Please note that pepper is at no time mentioned. It is most definitely out, and the sooner you lose your taste for it the better. Incidentally, I was never so happy as when I discovered how to peel garlic without touching it. You simply give it a good whack with the flat side of your big knife or cleaver and the skin simply parts from the clove. Certain seasonings, such as the above and soy sauce, may be used indiscriminately; spices should be used very sparingly, very rarely, if at all—substitute herbs. However, in the beginning keep your entire diet pure and simple —you can launch into variations on the theme next year!

Chances are you'll remain more or less on this regime for the rest of your life, as I certainly intend to. Therefore, common sense is of the utmost importance. You wouldn't be doing this if you weren't troubled by arthritis to some degree; if you're in terrible shape you'll obviously follow the diet to the letter, eschewing everything that is the least bit harmful. On the other hand, for some who feel remarkably better in a year or so it would seem reasonable to occasionally add a few goodies —things like a little dash of sherry in a sauce and a pinch of curry powder in a soup. Chicken broth, which I use throughout the book as a stock for soups and cooking, should not be used in the very beginning but may be added occasionally later. I now use it quite often with absolutely no ill effect. The same holds true for the white meat of chicken. I had been on the regime for a year and a half before I added, again occasionally, the white meat of chicken breasts. And did it taste good!

Flour of any kind is acceptable. However, very often I substitute corn starch. And I use arrowroot if I want a clear glaze-like sauce.

Sugar is, of course, perfectly acceptable, though fattening! Honey is a fine food, and the perfect substitute for preserves.

Remember that it's only the yolk of the egg you must eschew; egg whites are not only acceptable (the only acceptable dairy product), but a fine source of protein. With a little practice you can make a nice omelet from the white alone. It's possible, however, to make a quite acceptable substitute for the yolk of an egg. Take one large tablespoonful of soybean flour, mix it with half a cup of water. Boil till it thickens, stirring constantly, and strain into a bowl. Beat in soybean oil gradually until it's very thick, and add a pinch of salt. You can use this wherever you'd need the yolk of an egg, since it has much the same properties and flavor.

You can also make your own soy milk, and use it either for drinking (if you find the beany flavor palatable) or for cooking. Simply soak a cup of soybeans overnight, drain them, and grind them up in the blender. Add 9 cups of water, simmer for about half an hour, and drain out the solids through cheesecloth.

Remember, just about any idiot can be a good cook using masses of butter and thick cream. And spicy seasons can cover an army of cooking sins. There's real challenge in producing tempting, tasty fare while at the same time maintaining a rigid diet.

In general the recipes given in this book will serve from four to six, but the basic number of servings should be quite clear in every recipe. Only you will know about your appetite and that of your guests; by the same token, only you will know if one piece of a certain fish will serve one or two.

The first hurdle is one of attitude, isn't it? Habit is so strong, and at first you miss those old familiar foods. There will be a few days of feeling somewhat deprived; then well-being begins to take over and suddenly you decide it's all eminently worthwhile.

DO'S AND DON'TS

DO EAT

All seafoods
All vegetables, including avocados
Vegetable oils, particularly safflower and corn
Margarine free of milk solids, such as Mazola
Egg whites
Honey
Nuts, sunflower seeds, soybean products
Rice of all kinds: brown, white, wild

Bread to which nothing listed below has been added
Tea and coffee
Plain soda water
Parsley, onions, garlic, bay leaf, salt
Any kind of flour
Sugar

DO NOT EAT

Meat in any form, including broth
Fruit of any kind, including tomatoes
Dairy products, including egg yolks, milk, cheese, yogurt
Vinegar, or any other acid
Pepper (definitely)
Chocolate
Dry roasted nuts (the process involves monosodium glutamate)
Alcoholic beverages
Soft drinks (I have never found one without additives)
All additives, preservatives, chemicals, most especially monosodium glutamate. One exception to this rule is the lecithin in margarine.

PERHAPS OCCASIONALLY

Breast of chicken and chicken broth
A small amount of wine in cooking
A small drink of bourbon
A small pinch of spicy seasoning such as curry powder
Noodles or spaghetti, since the amount of egg is relatively small and somewhat broken down in the cooking

EXCEPTIONS

Persons who have gout, or who have been diagnosed as having what is called gouty arthritis, will do well to avoid certain things. This sensitivity must be determined by the individual, since it varies from person to person, but in general mushrooms, asparagus, spinach, artichokes, peas, and beans are possible offenders. As for alcohol, bourbon does not seem to be right for some people with gout; I would suggest vodka for their rare indulgence.

4

Appetizers

THESE ARE THINGS to serve with those cocktails
you don't drink but your friends most probably do.
There are times when you want to have people in
for something less than dinner, and some of these
will serve the purpose. I always have a tray of raw
vegetables for the many friends who are watching
the calories, and I like to serve one hot canapé. (It
looks as if you tried a little harder!)

CRUDITÉS

Cauliflower, broken into flowerettes
Carrot sticks
Green-pepper slices
Radishes, peeled back to flowers
Green onions
Small, fresh, raw, button mushrooms

Soak the raw vegetables in salted water in the
refrigerator, and arrange in mounds on a large

serving dish, with a dip in the center of safflower
oil mayonnaise mixed with soy sauce and some
chopped chives and parsley.

GUACAMOLE

1 large, very ripe avocado
¼ teaspoon salt
3 teaspoons minced or grated onion

Mix well and serve with tortillas or the raw vegetables listed in the previous recipe.

PIROSHKI

These delicious little Russian turnovers are quite
sensational, and well worth the trouble of doing
the pastry.

¼ cup minced onion
2 tablespoons margarine
1 cup chopped, cooked fish
¼ teaspoon crushed dill seed
2 tablespoons minced parsley

Sauté the onion in the margarine, add the other
ingredients, and if the mixture seems too dry add
a little water. Place it in the center of the following pastry, and fold over and patiently press the
edges together until you're sure they'll stay.

2 cups flour
1 teaspoon salt
⅔ cup margarine
⅔ cup water

Roll out thin and cut in 3-inch rounds; put in your filling; dampen the edges and press together firmly. Brush lightly with melted margarine and bake in a 400-degree oven until nicely browned.

SHRIMP PUFFS

⅔ cup chopped, cooked shrimp
1 egg white, stiffly beaten
½ cup safflower oil mayonnaise
¼ teaspoon salt

Fold the egg white into the ingredients; pile the mixture onto thin slices of French bread, toasted, put under the broiler until puffed and browned.

ARTICHOKE LEAVES WITH SHRIMP

Cook a nice large artichoke, separate the leaves and arrange on each leaf a few small, cooked shrimp which have been moistened with a little safflower oil mayonnaise.

ARTICHOKE BOTTOMS

Fill artichoke bottoms with small shrimp mixed with safflower oil mayonnaise, or with crab legs.

Olympia oysters are wonderful to use this way if you can get them. Minced clams mixed with a little diced celery and moistened with mayonnaise are also good.

EGGPLANT CAVIAR

1 baked eggplant, pared, seeded, and mashed
1 green pepper, seeded and chopped
1 onion, chopped
1 clove of garlic, crushed
3 tablespoons olive oil

Sauté the pepper and onion in the olive oil; add the garlic and eggplant. Salt to taste, and serve cold with crisp, thin wedges of toasted French bread.

SCALLOP PUFFS

1 pound sea scallops
¼ cup safflower oil mayonnaise
1 tablespoon minced parsley
½ teaspoon soy sauce
1 egg white, stiffly beaten

Simmer the scallops in about a cup of water in a covered pan for just a few minutes. Drain, cool, and cut in halves. Mix the mayonnaise with the parsley and soy sauce; beat the egg white and fold it in. Place the scallop halves on a baking sheet, top each with some of the mixture and brown under the broiler.

GARLIC OLIVES

Drain the juice from a can of large, black olives. Put them in a jar with 3 cloves crushed garlic, cover them with olive oil, and let them stand several days. Green olives are good prepared this way too, but first crush them slightly. Black olives served heated are a pleasant surprise.

MACADAMIA NUTS

These are delicious when roasted in a slow oven till brown and served hot.

5

Soups

I HAVE FOUND soups to be a very important part of my menu. The very form lends itself so admirably to the use of vegetables; the quantities and varieties are practically infinite.

First, it's imperative that you own a blender. If you've never had one, you'll find that experimentation with it opens a whole new field in cooking. You'll never wonder what to do with leftovers again!

Second, try to keep on hand a supply of chicken stock (to be used cautiously) and of court bouillon (see page 59)—homemade, because all canned varieties that I know of have harmful additives. Read that label! For some soups I use clam juice, and for some the water the vegetables were cooked in. I keep a jar of vegetable water in my refrigerator; and sometimes a combination of, say, the water peas were cooked in and the water beets were cooked in will produce an unusual and interesting flavor.

When choosing a soup bear in mind the vegetables that are particularly high in the vitamins and minerals suspected to relieve arthritis. Green vegetables, particularly cabbage, and potatoes will make a rich, healthy soup for you. Potatoes are good to use as thickener for a creamy-type soup. Onions are also beneficial, as is garlic. And then of course there are all the seafood soups . . . delicious, hearty, full of protein and all those natural minerals and vitamins from the sea that we have not as yet been able to ruin.

When you peer in the refrigerator and find leftover vegetables, rice, or potatoes, you have a soup started. All you need to do is put them in the blender with stock or water and add a few herbs or garlic salt. For instance, the other day I wanted a soup for lunch in cool weather. Checking the refrigerator, I turned up some leftover peas and a jar of chicken stock left from poaching some chicken breasts the night before. (This makes a lovely rich stock.)

I boiled a potato with a bunch of green onions, squeezed in a clove of garlic, put it through the blender, and added the stock. Just before serving I added some frozen shrimp. It was delicious, a real "homemade" soup, but I'd just made it up as I went along, adding and tasting. I've found you really can't go very far wrong when the ingredients are good, natural, and fresh to start with.

So experiment! Cook extra beets so you'll have some left over for borscht, use that extra rice as a thickener, and if you happen to be lucky enough to have leftover wild rice just stir it into a soup after it's been blended. Leftover fish can be used if it's been poached and filleted. In this case your stock would be either the court bouillon you have on hand or clam juice from the shelf.

CREAMY OYSTER SOUP

½ cup diced celery
1 clove garlic, crushed
1 bunch scallions, chopped
1 potato, diced
A 12-ounce can clam juice
1 can (about 10 ounces) small oysters
Parsley, chopped

Simmer the vegetables in the clam juice until very tender. Put through the blender, salt to taste, and add more clam juice if too thick. Add the oysters, heat, and serve immediately, sprinkled with the parsley.

LEEK AND POTATO SOUP

1 bunch leeks, cut up (white part only)
2 medium potatoes, diced
4 cups water
Salt
Tiny dash nutmeg
Chives, chopped

Sauté the leeks in margarine, add the other ingredients, and simmer till tender. Season, put through the blender, and serve sprinkled with the chives. Delicious cold, a mock vichyssoise.

FRESH PEA SOUP

Two 10-ounce packages frozen peas (or equivalent amount of fresh)
2 or 3 medium potatoes, diced
2 large onions, coarsely chopped
Fat pinch sugar
Fat pinch salt
Pinch nutmeg

Cook the peas as directed on the package, adding
a fat pinch of sugar as well as salt. Boil the onions
and potatoes in water to cover, and when tender
combine with the peas and a small amount of
margarine in the blender. Thin with water as
necessary, and season with salt and a pinch of
nutmeg.

GARLIC SOUP
(Wonderful for colds and flu)

1 large head garlic, very fresh
2 quarts chicken broth
1 quart water
2 cloves
½ bay leaf, pinch sage and thyme
4 sprigs parsley
3 cups diced potatoes
Handful stuffed green olives
3 tablespoons olive oil

Separate the garlic cloves and peel by laying on a
cutting board and slapping hard with the flat side
of a large-bladed knife or cleaver. The skin will

fall away. Combine the garlic, water, cloves, herbs, and olive oil; simmer in the chicken broth, covered, 30 minutes. Add the potatoes and simmer another 20 minutes. Put through the blender, reheat, and serve with olives sliced on top.

Variation: Leave out the potatoes but simmer the additional time and pour over a thick slice of toasted French bread in each bowl.

MUSHROOM SOUP

½ pound mushrooms, finely chopped
1 small onion, finely chopped
Heaping teaspoon flour
3 cups water
2 tablespoons margarine

Sauté the mushrooms and onion in the margarine, blend in the flour, and add the water. Simmer about 10 minutes.

CRAB BISQUE

½ cup frozen lima beans
½ cup sliced crookneck squash
2 stalks celery, scraped and sliced
⅓ cup crab meat, cooked or canned
Dash paprika

Cover the vegetables with water and simmer till tender. Add the crab meat and put through the blender. Sprinkle with the paprika; reheat.

CHINESE CABBAGE SOUP

    2 carrots, chopped
    Small bunch parsley, minced
    1 onion, finely chopped
    ½ head cabbage, finely chopped
    4 tablespoons margarine
    Salt
    1 quart water
    Soy sauce

Sauté the vegetables in the margarine till tender; add water and simmer 30 minutes. Just before serving add soy sauce to taste.

BROWN BEAN SOUP

    A 16-ounce package kidney beans
    1 quart water
    An 8-ounce package soupgreens

Sauté the soup vegetables in margarine, boil the beans in the water according to the directions on the package (about 1½ hours), put everything through the blender, and salt to taste.

FAKE BONGO BONGO SOUP

    1 jar (about 10 ounces) oysters, fresh
    ¼ of a 12-ounce package frozen spinach
    Tiny dash A-1 sauce
    Garlic salt to taste

Cook the spinach in 1 cup water till tender, add all the other ingredients, and put through the blender. Pour into ovenproof cups and top with a small drift of beaten egg white; put under the broiler till browned.

BOUILLABAISSE

This wonderful Mediterranean feast can be made from many different assortments of fish and shellfish. It more or less depends on what is available to you. Haddock, halibut, sea bass, whiting, perch, red snapper, trout, flounder, are all suitable for the fish part, and must be fresh, while the clams, scallops, crab, lobster, shrimp, and mussels can be fresh (preferably, of course) or frozen. The following version will give you an idea of the proportions.

2 pounds haddock, halibut, sea bass, etc.
1 quart water
½ cup olive oil
Thyme
Bay leaf
Fennel
2 tablespoons minced parsley
2 onions, chopped
1 clove garlic, crushed
½ green pepper, seeded and chopped
8 oysters
8 mussels
8 clams
1 cup crab meat
1 cup lobster meat
1 cup shelled shrimp
½ cup sliced pimentos
Tiny pinch saffron

Boil the cleaned fish in the water until the water is reduced by half; save the broth; cut the fish into serving pieces. Place the olive oil in a heavy soup pot with the onions, garlic, pepper, and herbs; add the broth and boil rapidly 5 minutes. Add the fish and simmer about an hour; add the rest of the seafood and the pimentos, and simmer another 10 minutes. Crumble the saffron into the soup and stir gently to distribute. Serve with crusty garlic French bread.

STEAMED CLAMS AND BROTH

Wash enough fresh clams for one person (about 6 to 8 clams) in cold running water. Put in a saucepan with ½ cup water, a pinch of bay leaf, and parsley and salt. Cover tightly; steam about 8 minutes or until all the clams are open. Pour the broth in a cup, add a piece of margarine, and dunk the clams in more melted, salted margarine.

MEDITERRANEAN VEGETABLE SOUP

3 or 4 potatoes, diced
1 pound fresh green beans, trimmed
½ pound spaghetti
3 cloves garlic
¼ cup olive oil
Small handful fresh basil leaves, or heaping
    tablespoon dried

Cook the vegetables in 1½ quarts water, salted well. When they are almost tender, break the spaghetti into the pot and finish cooking very slowly. Grind the basil, garlic, and oil in a mortar and pestle and mix into the soup.

VEGETABLE SOUP

1 leek, scrubbed and sliced thin
1 medium onion, cubed
1 small, white turnip, cubed
2 carrots, diced
½ cup sliced celery
½ cup chopped parsley
3 tablespoons margarine
3 potatoes, cubed
1½ teaspoons salt

Place all the ingredients except the potatoes and salt in a pot; cook, stirring, 3 or 4 minutes. Then add the potatoes and salt and about 2 quarts water; cook about 1 hour, or until the vegetables are tender. Serve with a sprinkle of minced parsley.

WATERCRESS SOUP

Put a large, fresh bunch of watercress, stems and all, in a pot with a cut-up potato and a bunch of sliced leeks. Add about a quart of water; salt well and simmer till the potato is tender. Put through the blender a very few seconds, just enough to chop the watercress but not enough to purée.

GARDEN SOUP

This is a more elaborate soup using watercress. It uses many of the same ingredients as my other soups, but this particular combination produces a uniquely elegant and delicate soup to serve, for instance, before a rather elaborate dinner.

> 1 bunch watercress
> ½ head iceberg lettuce
> 4 scallions, *all* of them
> 4 outside cabbage leaves
> Bunch parsley
> Sprig fresh thyme, if possible (or substitute pinch of powdered)
> Quart chicken broth
> Salt

Chop the vegetables fine; sauté, stirring, in margarine about 10 minutes. Add the broth; cover and simmer 30 minutes. Season with salt, and put through the blender; reheat.

ABALONE SOUP

> 1-pound can abalone
> 2 cups chicken stock
> 1 teaspoon soy sauce
> Dash sherry

Pour the juice from the can of abalone and add enough water to it to make 2 cups. Add to this the chicken stock, the soy sauce, the sherry, and ¼ cup of the abalone cut into matchstick pieces. Heat; salt to taste.

OLD-FASHIONED PEA SOUP

Start soaking 1 cup dried peas about 10:30 A.M. At 3:00 P.M. put them on to boil covered with a liberal supply of water. About 5:00 add a potato, finely diced, and a chopped onion. Add water when needed. Put the soup in a double boiler for one more hour.

SCALLOP CHOWDER

This is one of the few chowder recipes that taste like chowder without the inclusion of all the *verboten* ingredients like bacon or pork.

    1 pound sea scallops
    3 tablespoons margarine
    1 medium onion, chopped
    3 stalks celery, sliced
    1 quart boiling water
    ¼ green pepper, chopped
    6 medium yams, peeled and sliced in 1-inch
        pieces
    2 cups court bouillon (see page 59)
    2 teaspoons salt
    2 teaspoons cornstarch

Sauté the onion and celery in the margarine; add the boiling water, green pepper, yams, fish stock, and salt. Cook over medium heat 15 minutes; add the scallops and cook 10 minutes longer. Check the yams for tenderness; lastly stir in the cornstarch (which has been mixed with a little cold water).

AVOCADO BISQUE

1 large, ripe avocado
1 tablespoon minced onion
1 tablespoon margarine
1 tablespoon flour
2 cups chicken stock

Sauté the minced onion slowly in some margarine. Make a roux of the flour and the tablespoon of margarine and add the chicken stock gradually. Press the avocado through a sieve; add it to the onion and stir quickly for about half a minute. Add the stock and salt to taste. Serve hot with croutons.

JELLIED BORSCHT

2 cups beet juice (made from boiling about 4 beets in 1 quart water)
3 cups clam juice
3 whole cloves
1 medium onion, chopped
2 cabbage leaves
1 tablespoon unflavored gelatin in 2 tablespoons cold water

Combine the beet juice and clam juice with the cloves, onion, and cabbage leaves; simmer 10 minutes. Strain, and to the liquid add the gelatin mixed with water. This will make a thin jelly, and if you wish it thicker add more gelatin. Chill and serve sprinkled with a few dill seeds.

VICHYSSOISE

1 large potato
2 tablespoons margarine
1 medium onion, chopped
4 cups chicken broth
Dash nutmeg
Salt
Chives, finely cut

Cut the potato in cubes and simmer in the broth till done. Meanwhile sauté the onion in the margarine, being careful not to brown it; cover it with a lid and let it stand till the potato is done. Purée all together in the blender with the nutmeg and salt, chill for several hours, and serve topped with the chives. (This is quite a thick soup; if it seems too thick, thin it with a little water.)

COLD CUCUMBER SOUP

1 very large or 2 small cucumbers
6 ounces clam juice
Pinch curry powder

Peel and dice the cucumber and put everything in the blender. Purée and serve very cold.

CLAM BROTH WITH DICED AVOCADO

Combine a 12-ounce can or bottle clam juice with 2 cups chicken broth, and serve with diced avocado floating in it.

CLAM BROTH WITH CELERY

Make a celery broth from the leaves of celery, add an equal part of clam juice, and serve with finely chopped celery in it.

OYSTER STEW

1 pint oysters
¼ cup margarine
½ cup finely chopped celery
3 cups chicken stock
Parsley or chervil, chopped
Salt to taste

Cook the oysters and celery in the margarine about 3 minutes. Add the chicken stock, and when hot salt to taste and serve spinkled with the chervil or parsley.

CREAM OF ONION SOUP

3 large, sweet Spanish onions, sliced thin
2 cups clam juice
1 cup water
2 medium potatoes, sliced
1½ tablespoons margarine
1 cup chopped Spanish onion
1 tablespoon cornstarch
1 teaspoon salt
Chopped parsley

Cook the onion slices in the liquid 20 minutes. If you prefer, you may substitute chicken broth for the clam juice. I must remind you here that the chicken broth you use is an occasional goody, not something for the daily menu. Add the potatoes and salt and cook 15 minutes longer; purée in the blender. Sauté the chopped onion in the margarine until golden; blend in the cornstarch, which has been mixed with a little cold water; add this to the puréed mixture and bring to a boil, thinning with clam juice if too thick. Sprinkle on the chopped parsley before serving.

ONION SOUP

3 tablespoons margarine
3 cups chopped onion
2 tablespoons flour
6 cups water
1 bay leaf
Salt to taste
French bread

Sauté the onion in the margarine till browned; blend in the flour. Stir in the water gradually, add the bay leaf and salt, and cook over low heat 30 minutes. Throw out the bay leaf. Place a slice of toasted French bread in each bowl and pour the soup over it.

FRENCH SEAFOOD BISQUE

This is a divine rich mixture of seafood. It makes a wonderful winter luncheon dish.

>   5 tablespoons margarine
>   2 tablespoons each minced parsley, onion, carrot, celery
>   ½ pound cooked crab or lobster meat (fresh, frozen, or canned), coarsely chopped
>   ½ pound cooked shrimp, coarsely chopped
>   An 8-ounce can minced clams
>   3 cups clam juice
>   ¼ cup dry white wine (it adds so much to this soup, and the harm is almost cooked out)
>   ½ teaspoon thyme
>   2 tablespoons cornstarch
>   Salt
>   Pinch nutmeg

Sauté the minced vegetables in 2 tablespoons of the margarine until soft. Add the crab, shrimp, clams and liquid from can, wine, and thyme. Heat about 5 minutes without allowing to boil. Make a roux of the remaining 3 tablespoons of margarine and the cornstarch (which has been mixed with a little cold water), and gradually add the liquid from the seafood pan. Stir until thickened, and season with salt and nutmeg. Put about half the seafood mixture in the blender for just a few seconds; then combine all the ingredients and reheat before serving.

CREAM OF ALMOND SOUP

1 cup blanched almonds
1 quart chicken broth
Bouquet of 3 sprigs parsley, 2 sprigs thyme, 1
    piece celery tied together, and 1 chopped
    onion
2 tablespoons margarine
2 tablespoons cornstarch

Grate the almonds in the blender; combine them
with the broth, bouquet, and onion in a pan; simmer 30 minutes. Discard the bouquet. In another
pan melt the margarine; stir in the cornstarch
mixed with a little water; add a little of the soup
mixture till thickened; then put everything together; boil and stir 1 minute; and taste for seasoning. Garnish with toasted, slivered almonds.

PEASANT VEGETABLE SOUP

2 carrots, scraped and sliced
3 leeks, thinly sliced
1 parsnip, peeled and thinly sliced
1½ cups chopped cabbage
3 tablespoons margarine
8 cups water
1 bay leaf
A 10- or 12-ounce package frozen mixed vege-
    tables
¼ cup rice
1 cup chopped spinach
1 cup chopped lettuce

Sauté the carrots, leeks, parsnip, and cabbage in the margarine. Add the water, bay leaf, mixed vegetables, and rice. Cook covered over low heat 20 minutes or until the rice is done; then add the spinach and lettuce and cook 5 minutes. Salt to taste.

GREENS SOUP

½ cup chopped scallions
4 tablespoons margarine
2 cups diced potatoes
4 cups water
1 cup watercress
1 cup chopped lettuce
1 cup spinach or sorrel

Sauté the scallions in margarine 5 minutes. Add the potatoes, water, watercress, lettuce, and spinach. Cover and cook 15 minutes over low heat. Put through the blender and stir in a dollop of margarine; salt to taste.

NEW ORLEANS GUMBO

½ pound shrimp
1 quart water
1 tablespoon margarine
1 small onion, minced
1 clove garlic, minced
1 stalk celery, chopped
1 bay leaf
2 sprigs parsley, chopped
½ teaspoon thyme
1 tablespoon cornstarch
¼ cup water
½ pint oysters
1 teaspoon file powder

Shell the shrimp. Boil the shells 10 minutes; discard the shells; add water to make a quart. Brown the onion, garlic, celery, bay leaf, parsley, and thyme in the margarine. Add them to the stock, thicken with cornstarch softened in water, and boil 1 hour. Add the shrimp and oysters, cooking gently till the oysters curl. Add file powder just before serving.

COURT BOUILLON

You will need this stock for many recipes in this book. You can make it ahead and keep it in a jar in the refrigerator for up to a week.

2 pounds fish trimmings
2 quarts water
1 bay leaf
¼ pound margarine
2 carrots, sliced
3 stalks celery, chopped
1 large onion, sliced
Pinch thyme
3 sprigs parsley
2 teaspoons salt

Boil everything together for 1 hour; strain.

VEGETABLE SOUP PROVENÇAL

1 pound zucchini
½ teaspoon salt
1½ cups chopped onion
1 clove garlic
2 cups fresh lima beans
6 cups water
1 cup fresh peas
4 cloves garlic
Handful parsley
Handful basil
2 tablespoons olive oil mixed with safflower oil
½ cup safflower oil mayonnaise

Grate the zucchini and add the salt; let set awhile, then put through the blender, with the juice. Sauté the onions and 1 clove garlic in margarine till translucent but not browned; add the zucchini and sauté a few more minutes. Now add the lima beans to the water; boil till almost done and add the peas. Put through the blender and add to the zucchini-onion mixture.

Serve topped with a large spoonful of this version of *pistou:* Crush 4 cloves garlic in a pestle with the parsley and basil. Add the oil to the mixture as you grind, and when smooth add the mayonnaise. Serve this soup with some nice homemade French bread!

MINESTRONE

¼ pound white beans
½ pound zucchini
1 medium potato
3 cups cabbage, cut in small strips
¼ pound green string beans, cut in small pieces
2 quarts water
2 tablespoons olive oil
4 tablespoons chopped onions
1 clove garlic, crushed
¼ cup rice
3 tablespoons chopped parsley
Salt and basil to taste

Pour boiling water over the white beans and let stand 2 hours. Drain. Put them in the 2 quarts water and cook 1 hour. Sauté the onions in the oil; peel and dice the potato and zucchini, add them to the onion mixture, and sauté 5 more minutes. Add them to the white beans; then add the green beans, cabbage, garlic, salt, and basil. Cover and cook over low heat 1¼ hours. Add the rice and chopped parsley and cook 20 minutes more, or until the rice is done.

6

Salads

As BREAD is my breakfast, so salad seems to have become my daily luncheon. Drawing from the lettuce crisper and the canned goods shelf, I always have my ingredients at hand, quick and easy to fix. And most important, I can always find a salad on a restaurant menu and know that the ingredients haven't been tampered with in the kitchen. I simply ask for an oil dressing—skip the vinegar, please! And I particularly like garlic salt, so I find an oil-garlic salt dressing very palatable.

Leftover cooked vegetables are delicious in salads. One can make all kinds of variations on, say, the Salade Niçoise (see page 63) by cleaning out the refrigerator. Tuna fish, the solid white albacore kind, is a mainstay, and Saffola or another safflower oil mayonnaise is delicious when mixed with a little soy sauce and a squeeze of garlic.

Another wonderful dressing is made with shallots—admittedly not always easy to get but well worth it for their subtle, gentle, oniony flavor

tinged with garlic. Peel and slice them very thin,
and add them to your oil with salt. This is a great
dressing for raw or very slightly cooked vegetable
salads. It's best if allowed to marinate awhile before being served.

In preparing vegetables for salad, some such as
zucchini and mushrooms should be sliced thinly
and served raw; green beans, carrots, beets, and
the like should be cooked till barely done and then
sliced. Run cold water over them to cool immediately after cooking.

SALADE NIÇOISE

New potatoes, boiled whole
Green beans, cooked crisp
Beets, cooked or canned
Tuna, the best chunky white albacore
Anchovies and black olives

Chill all the ingredients and arrange on a bed of
lettuce in the desired proportions. Decorate with
strips of anchovies and olives. Crush 1 clove garlic
in ½ cup olive oil, add a touch of dry mustard and
lots of salt, and pour over salad.

ASPARAGUS SALAD

Another delicious salad plate, suitable for an entire luncheon, is based on fresh asparagus. Add
shrimp (cooked, shelled, and deveined), artichoke
hearts, and pitted ripe olives. Arrange them at-

tractively on lettuce and serve with an oil dressing to which you've added (mixed *very* well) a crushed clove of garlic, ½ teaspoon cumin seed, a pinch of dry mustard, a pinch of paprika, and about ⅛ teaspoon salt.

CHINESE SALAD

Two 8-ounce bunches spinach
¼ cup oil
½ pound small shrimp, such as San Francisco Bay shrimp, available canned
2 tablespoons soy sauce

Cook the spinach; rinse in ice-cold water; chop. Combine the oil, soy sauce, and shrimp and add to the spinach. Serve very cold.

ENDIVE AND BEET SALAD

Chop endive and cooked beets, toss together in oil, and salt to taste.

SARAH BERNHARDT SALAD

Line a salad bowl with leaves of lettuce and in the center make a bed of shredded lettuce. Place a bunch of asparagus tips upright in the center and surround it with artichoke bottoms and mounds of minced celery mixed with safflower oil mayonnaise. Pour over this a dressing made of olive oil seasoned with a little soy sauce and garlic salt.

RUSSIAN SALAD I

Place three artichoke bottoms on a bed of watercress; fill one with shrimp and diced celery, mixed with safflower oil mayonnaise; one with rolled anchovies sprinkled with chopped chives; and one with diced sardines, crab flakes, and caviar. Serve with olive oil and onion salt. This very fancy version makes a lovely first course for a dinner party or buffet.

RUSSIAN SALAD II

This is a delicious, healthy version in which you can use almost any combination of vegetables. Line a bowl with lettuce; place mounds of diced beets, potatoes, string beans, and peas around a small head of cauliflower in the center. I like all the vegetables cooked *al dente*, crisp and chilled. Serve with safflower oil mayonnaise mixed with ¼ cup soy sauce.

AVOCADOS

We prefer to eat avocados the epicurean way. Simply cut the avocado in half, remove the seed, and place it on a few lettuce leaves or a bed of watercress. Sprinkle the avocado with a few drops of oil and salt and eat it with a spoon.

CELERY-HEART SALAD

Celery hearts are only available at certain times of the year, but they are well worth the trouble of boiling till tender and peeling away all the dark outside. Dice the white part, mix with oil and garlic salt, and serve on watercress.

CUCUMBER AND WATERCRESS SALAD

This salad is made in the proportions of ⅓ watercress to ⅔ cucumbers cut in ½-inch dice; it's a good combination served with oil and garlic salt or safflower oil mayonnaise.

CELERY-HEART AND AVOCADO SALAD

On a nest of romaine lettuce arrange slices of avocado alternated with pieces of celery heart cut as nearly as possible the same size. Garnish with julienned beets and parsley, and serve with olive oil and salt.

MUSHROOM AND FENNEL SALAD

1½ pounds fresh mushrooms
3 fennel hearts or celery hearts
½ cup safflower oil mayonnaise
1 tablespoon mustard
3 tablespoons oil
Salt

Wipe the mushrooms after washing thoroughly. Chop them together with the fennel until very fine. Make a dressing of the other ingredients and serve on a bed of lettuce.

CUCUMBER AND MUSHROOM ASPIC

2 cups water
2 bay leaves, crumbled
2 teaspoons tarragon
Celery salt
2 packages unflavored gelatin, softened in a little cold water
1 teaspoon grated onion
1¼ cups ice cubes and water
1¼ cups peeled cucumber
1½ cups sliced fresh mushrooms
¼ cup pimento strips
Salad greens, cold and crisp

Bring to a boil the water, bay leaves, tarragon, and celery salt. Pour this over the gelatin; stir until dissolved. Let stand 5 minutes; strain; add onion, ice cubes, and water. Stir until the ice melts; chill till very thick. Peel and flute the cucumbers; stem the mushrooms; blot both with paper towels; then slice the mushrooms lengthwise. With the pimento, fold them into the gelatin. Chill in a 2-quart mold and serve turned out on a chilled plate surrounded by crisp greens.

CLAM SALAD

This doesn't sound too terribly good, but it is. I invented it one day when I couldn't find anything but these ingredients for lunch.

> 8-ounce can chopped clams (not the minced variety)
> Several stalks tender celery, diced
> 3 scallions with a little of the green top
> About ¼ green pepper, cut in slivers
> Safflower oil mayonnaise

Drain the clams but not too thoroughly, so that you retain just a little of their juice. Mix all the ingredients together with just enough mayonnaise to hold it together and season to taste. Serve on a crisp bed of lettuce.

CALIFORNIA SALAD

> 1 cup sliced fresh mushrooms
> 1 cup cooked baby shrimp
> 1 teaspoon tarragon
> About ⅓ cup olive oil
> Ripe chilled avocados
> Crisp lettuce

Combine the mushrooms, shrimp, tarragon, and oil; salt generously. Chill in the refrigerator and serve in peeled, halved avocados on a bed of lettuce.

AIOLI

This is used in Provence in many ways, but I find it delicious with fresh cooked or raw vegetables. It can be served in a bowl with the vegetables surrounding it in separate dishes, or it can be used simply as an adjunct to the vegetable served with the main course.

6 cloves garlic, peeled and crushed
1 cup safflower oil mayonnaise
¼ cup olive oil
Salt

Add the garlic to the mayonnaise; add the oil little by little.

MOLDED TUNA SALAD

1 tablespoon unflavored gelatin, softened in a little cold water
¼ cup cold clam juice
¼ cup hot chicken stock
¾ cup safflower oil mayonnaise
1 cup flaked albacore tuna
2 tablespoons chopped ripe olives
¼ cup slivered, blanched almonds
Chopped celery, walnuts, pimento to taste

Mix everything together and chill in a 9-inch rin
mold for fish or any other mold.

LOBSTER-TAIL SALAD

Lobster tails are so flavorful that they need littl
dressing up. Drop the frozen tails in salted boilin;
water with a bay leaf for about 5 minutes; drai
and chill. Cut into salad-size pieces and marinat
in olive oil, dill, and chopped parsley for severa
hours. Serve on crisp lettuce.

FISH SALAD

This is served at a Greek restaurant in London
the White Tower. It is served in variations al
around the Mediterranean, and makes a perfec
summer luncheon dish.

> 1 pound firm white fish (such as turbot)
>   poached, drained, and chilled
> ¼ cup chopped onion
> ¼ cup chopped parsley
> 1 large bay leaf, finely crumbled
> About ⅓ cup olive oil
> Salt

Cut the fish into neat bite-sized cubes; marinate
with dressing made from the other ingredients.
Serve slivered celery root on the side.

CHICKEN SALAD

2 cups diced, cooked chicken breasts
1 cup diced celery
4 scallions, including some tops, minced
1 teaspoon chopped dill or basil
1 cup safflower oil mayonnaise
½ cucumber, peeled and diced

Mix everything together and serve very cold on crisp romaine leaves.

COLESLAW

This is probably the most important of the salads. It just could not be better for you! Make it often! Shred raw cabbage and soak it in ice water in the refrigerator for an hour or so before using. Drain and dry carefully, blotting and turning in paper towels. Add lots of thinly sliced green pepper, grated onion, and, if desired, grated raw carrot. Add some dill weed if you like, lots of salt, and a small amount of salad oil. Bind everything together with safflower oil mayonnaise.

SCANDINAVIAN HERRING SALAD

2 large salt herrings
2½ cups diced, boiled potatoes
2 cups diced beets
½ onion, chopped
2 tablespoons oil
½ cup safflower oil mayonnaise

Wash the herrings; cut off the heads and tails and soak in cold water overnight. Drain and fillet; dice the fillets, carefully removing any skin. Toss everything carefully so as not to break the potatoes and beets; chill thoroughly; serve on crisp lettuce.

GREEN SALAD WITH CROUTONS

With all the different sorts of lettuce available there's no reason not to have lots of variety. Escarole and romaine make a nice combination and with the addition of some sliced cucumbers and croutons you have a rather different green salad. For the croutons, make cubes of leftover French bread and sauté them in olive oil in which you have crushed a clove of garlic. It goes without saying, I hope, that you always dry your lettuce most carefully, patting each leaf if necessary. A French wire lettuce basket that you swing is great but requires a back-door area unless you don't mind a little rain in your kitchen.

SHRIMP SALAD WITH RICE AND PEAS

Here is a delicious salad, complete in all nutrients for a balanced meal.

Put the following in a heavy pan and simmer 30 minutes. (The bouquet garni should be in cheesecloth for easy removal.)

1 cup olive oil
3 cups water
½ cup soy sauce
½ teaspoon tabasco
Salt
Bouquet garni composed of:
    2 leeks or 6 scallions, cut in pieces
    1 teaspoon tarragon
    Bunch celery leaves
    Handful parsley
    3 cloves
    Small piece of cinnamon stick

Now add about 3 pounds raw, peeled, and deveined shrimp and bring back to a boil. After about 10 seconds remove from the stove and let stand till cool. Refrigerate overnight. The following day remove the shrimp with a slotted spoon and boil the marinade down to about 2 cups. Add about 2 tablespoons cornstarch very carefully (mixed with a little cold water first, of course) and then fold in 3 stiffly beaten egg whites.

Meanwhile you have cooked and drained 2 cups rice; while the rice is still warm mix in salt, a pinch of nutmeg, a bunch of finely chopped scallions, and several tablespoons olive oil.

With your other hand you've put in a pan ½ stick margarine, about 2 tablespoons finely minced onion, and ½ cup water. Cook until the water has boiled away and the onion is soft. Stir in 1 package frozen peas (over which hot water has been poured to defrost); mix well; and you're ready to serve. Mound the peas in the center of a round platter, make a ring of rice around them, add a ring of shrimp around that, and decorate the edge with attractive lettuce leaves, watercress, or parsley. Serve the sauce separately.

CRAB LOUIS

This is another hearty lunch salad, and of course a particular favorite of any San Franciscan.

Use whatever crab you can get—fresh crab is available on the West Coast—but if you can't get anything else the frozen Dungeness is delicious. Arrange the crab meat on a crisp, cold bed of lettuce and cover with the following dressing.

2 cups safflower oil mayonnaise
½ cup finely chopped scallions
½ cup finely chopped seeded green pepper
¼ cup soy sauce
Salt to taste

AVOCADO MOUSSE

3 cups mashed avocado (about 5 very ripe avocados)
2 tablespoons unflavored gelatin in ½ cup cold water
½ cup boiling water
½ teaspoon onion powder
1 teaspoon salt
Dash tabasco
2 tablespoons minced parsley
½ cup safflower oil mayonnaise

Soak the gelatin in cold water 5 minutes; dissolve in the boiling water. Put the avocado in the blender with the parsley and everything but the mayonnaise. Then fold in the latter and pour the mixture into a quart mold which has been rinsed out with cold water. Chill till firm; mold on a bed of watercress.

GREEN GODDESS DRESSING

The old Palace Hotel in San Francisco is credited with this unusual dressing. It was reportedly invented for George Arliss when he was appearing here in a play titled *The Green Goddess*.

    8 anchovy fillets
    1 scallion
    Handful parsley
    8–10 leaves fresh tarragon, or 2 teaspoons dried
    ¼ cup chives
    3 cups safflower oil mayonnaise

Put everything in the blender and run till smooth. Serve cold over firm lettuce such as romaine or iceberg.

CAULIFLOWER SALAD

    2 cups cold, cooked cauliflower
    4 scallions, chopped
    1 green pepper, seeded and chopped
    2 anchovies, chopped
    ½ cup diced beets
    ½ cup safflower oil mayonnaise

Mix everything together and serve very cold on crisp lettuce leaves.

SALAD MIXTURES

Use your imagination with combinations like cold cauliflower, strips of green pepper, thinly sliced celery, scallions, and diced avocado. A can of chopped ripe olives is an interesting addition to a green salad. Broccoli and zucchini make a good combination served with oil and garlic salt.

CRAB-MEAT LUNCHEON PLATTER

Make a large bed of crisp lettuce in the center of the platter. In this place a mound of crab meat mixed with chopped celery and safflower oil mayonnaise. Around the crab meat make a rim of frozen baby lima beans which have been cooked and chilled in a marinade of olive oil and onion salt.

JELLIED CRAB-MEAT SALAD

1 tablespoon unflavored gelatin, softened in a little cold water
¼ cup hot water
¾ cup safflower oil mayonnaise
½ cup diced celery
2 tablespoons chopped green olives
½ green pepper, minced
½ teaspoon salt
1½ cups crab meat
2 tablespoons chopped pimentos

Soak the gelatin in the hot water 5 minutes. Add to the mayonnaise slowly; then immediately add the gelatin-mayonnaise mixture to all the other ingredients and chill in a ring mold.

CELERY VICTOR

Select uniform stalks of dwarf celery or hearts of celery. Wash, unseparated, and simmer in water and soy sauce (about 1 part sauce to 4 parts water) until tender. Drain carefully; marinate in olive oil, dill weed, and garlic salt for several hours before serving, chilled.

JELLIED CUCUMBER SALAD

3 teaspoons unflavored gelatin, softened in a
  little cold water
1 cup hot water
4 cucumbers, peeled and grated
1 tablespoon onion juice
¼ teaspoon salt

Dissolve the softened gelatin in the hot water.
When cool, add the remaining ingredients and
chill in a ring mold.

SCALLOPS IN CUCUMBERS

4–6 long cucumbers
½ cup diced celery
2 pimentos, chopped fine
½ green pepper, chopped fine
1 pound scallops, cooked and diced
2 tablespoons safflower oil mayonnaise
½ small onion, grated
Onion salt to taste

Peel the cucumbers and cut lengthwise; scoop out
the seeds and chill. Combine the celery, pimentos,
green pepper, scallops, mayonnaise, and onion.
Add onion salt to taste. Fill the cucumbers with
the mixture and serve on salad greens or watercress.

SCALLOP SALAD

2 pounds scallops
1 cup diced cucumber
1 cup thinly sliced celery
¼ cup sliced, stuffed green olives
1 cup safflower oil mayonnaise
A little oil to thin

Combine everything and serve on watercress.

ALMOND CUCUMBER SALAD

2 cucumbers, peeled and sliced very thin
½ teaspoon salt
1 cup safflower oil mayonnaise
¼ cup chopped, blanched, and toasted al-
     monds
2 tablespoons minced chives

Mix everything together, chill, and serve on leaves
of butter lettuce or an available substitute.

OLYMPIA OYSTER SALAD

1 pint Olympia oysters
Safflower oil mayonnaise to which has been
     added 1 finely chopped anchovy

Simmer oysters in their own liquor for a minute
or two. Chill and serve coated with mayonnaise on
a bed of lettuce.

HEARTS OF LETTUCE WITH
AVOCADO DRESSING

2 very ripe avocados
1 tablespoon grated onion
Salt to taste

Put the avocado through a blender, mix with onion, salt to taste, and serve on chilled lettuce hearts.

CHEF'S SALAD BOWL

I have a plastic salad bowl with a cover that I keep in the freezer. I take the icy-cold bowl from the freezer, put a salad together, all but the dressing, and have it crisping in the refrigerator while I do other things. Don't put the dressing on till you're ready to serve, however. This is my Sunday luncheon salad.

1 medium head romaine lettuce
¼ medium head Bibb lettuce
½ bunch chicory
¼ bunch watercress
2 cups shredded cabbage
1 cup small shrimp
1 cup breast of chicken cut in julienne strips
1 medium green pepper, cut in strips
6 green olives, chopped
1 bunch scallions, finely chopped

Break the greens into bite-size pieces; combine everything in a bowl, with the shrimp and chicken on top. When ready to serve pour over this a dressing of 1 cup safflower oil mayonnaise mixed with ¼ cup soy sauce and 2 cloves crushed garlic. Toss at the table.

SPINACH SALAD

1 tablespoon chopped white onion
2 tablespoons diced celery
1 teaspoon sliced green pepper
½ teaspoon chopped fresh parsley
Two 8-ounce bunches fresh, young spinach, washed and chilled
¼ cup olive oil
¼ teaspoon salt
Pinch dry mustard
¼ teaspoon oregano

Mince the onion, celery, green pepper, and parsley together until very fine and pulpy. Add the oil and seasonings and let stand for quite awhile to blend well. Pour this over the spinach leaves, which have been torn into small pieces, and toss.

7

Seafood

A GLANCE at the globe will tell you that the earth is predominantly covered with water. Is it any wonder, then, that whole populations have been living on fish since time began? There have been whole populations of healthy, vital, fish-eating people all through history, particularly seafarers such as the Vikings. Even today fish constitutes the major source of food for people all over the world; the exception is the affluent United States. The United States has the highest arthritic rate in the world!

Fish is a perfect source of protein, low in fats, high in minerals and vitamins. All seafood contains a supply of iron, magnesium, iodine, calcium, copper, phosphorus, and fluorides.

However, you may ask, "What about mercury pollution?" No one can be unaware of this subject. Mercury has been present in our seafood for thousands of years—probably, in fact, since the beginning of time—and admittedly the extreme toxicity of mercury has been recognized for over a thousand years, but recently dangerous industrial spillages have raised the question of safety.

Various opinions have been voiced, but I quote from some of our soundest experts. Dr. Leonard J. Goldwater—Professor of Community Health Services at Duke University, Visiting Professor in Environmental Sciences at the University of North Carolina, Professor Emeritus of Occupational Medicine at Columbia University, consultant to various groups such as the World Health Organization, the Environmental Protection Agency, and the fishing, canning, paint, and mercury industries—has some heartening things to say on the subject. His interest dates back to 1936, and he states that no case of mercury poisoning from seafood has ever been suspected in the United States or Canada; mercury poisoning has been limited to people who have existed on an unbalanced diet not intended for human consumption. Dr. Goldwater criticizes the instant experts and the "press-inspired hysteria over mercury in food fish" and says flatly that Americans can eat fish without fear of mercury poisoning. Dr. Thomas B. Eyl of St. Clair, Michigan, found no cases of mercury poisoning in a study of longtime heavy-to-moderate fish eaters whose fish came from a lake known to be polluted with mercury.

Published reports in recent years have found excess levels of mercury in some swordfish and canned tuna; you won't find recipes for swordfish or large tuna in this book. It seems that the retention of mercury increases in direct relation to the size of the fish. An article in the *Saturday Review* for February 6, 1971, states it this way:

The danger of mercury poisoning in fish generally increases with the size of the fish. To provide an adequate number of marketable cuts, swordfish must run upwards of 100 pounds in weight. Therefore the chances are high that swordfish will remain off the market in this country because of the mercury threat. There is a greater chance that tuna supplies will be less curtailed for the following reasons. Tuna meat is classified by its color, with the white meat of albacore the most popular, then the progressively darker meat of the yellow fin, the skipjack, the big eye, and the blue fin. Albacore average 45 pounds, yellow fin 150, big eye 235, blue fin even more.

Mercury has been used in medicine for centuries. Mercurial diuretics for kidney diseases are given in amounts many thousands of times greater than that found in fish, often with life-saving results. And incidentally, the mercury level in our cattle and other foodstuffs tends to make the seafood level look safer by comparison.

As to the availability of seafood, it's certainly easier if you're near one of our coasts . . . but with our modern transportation and facilities for quick freezing, fish is really obtainable by everyone. When purchasing fresh fish I find the advice of the local fish merchant to be my best guide. Almost all fish are somewhat seasonal and your fishman is the one to tell you what's best at the moment. For instance, here in California there's a season for salmon fishing, and when it opens on March 15 I'm first in line. Our crab is also seasonal, of course, and somewhat difficult to get . . . but anything that's so good shouldn't be too easy!

The East Coast has its own marvelous selection of delectable seafood, and their availability depends on locality. The West Coast has a somewhat different selection, but those available almost all year are bass, cod, halibut, lingcod, mackerel, rockfish, sablefish, smelt, sole, sturgeon, and our wonderful tiny shrimp. We also have our seasonal seafood, such as salmon, crab, abalone, and albacore (fresh tuna). A great number of these are available frozen, including prawns, oysters, and lobster tails, and of course frozen fish is the answer for those of you who are landlocked. It may be used in the same way as fresh.

When purchasing fish the primary thing, of course, is to make sure it's absolutely fresh. When you see it in the fish market or store it should be on ice, and it should have been there from the time it was caught. When you take it home it should be kept as cold as possible, without freezing, in your refrigerator. One way to judge freshness easily is that the fish simply does not smell objectionable . . . fishy, yes, but not objectionably so. When you press down on the fish it should spring back; the eyes should be clear and bright; the scales should still be shiny and colorful.

Allow a whole pound to a person when buying a whole fish, and when buying fillets or steaks allow between ⅓ and ½ pound depending on your appetites. In these portions you will be getting vitamin A, all the vitamin D you can use, and sometimes vitamin C, thiamine, riboflavin, and nicotinic acids, plus all those minerals I mentioned earlier!

Frozen fish are generally sold in the form of steaks or fillets. I have my best luck letting them thaw very slowly in the refrigerator, but of course this involves preplanning that is not always possible. In any case, always have your fish or shellfish completely thawed before cooking.

As a general rule, fish requires much more delicate cooking than any other protein source. Since it has no tough fibers to break down, it requires less time and when overcooked quickly becomes dried-out and tough. Testing with a fork for flaking, which means that the natural sectioning of the flesh of the fish separates easily, is the usual rule-of-thumb. Fish with a higher fat content—such as salmon, mackerel, and albacore—lend themselves best to broiling and baking; others such as sole and sea bass lend themselves well to poaching.

However, almost all fillets and steaks lend themselves to being sautéed, and to me this is one of the easiest and most delicious ways to serve fish. Simply take rather thin fillets or steaks, dredge them very lightly in flour, and pan-fry them in margarine for a very few minutes. (I usually mix a little corn oil in with the margarine . . . it seems to brown better without burning.) Broiled fish should generally be basted with the same combination, after the same flour-dusting treatment.

Fish such as fillet of sole or salmon steak, cooked easily and quickly this way, served with a baked potato and a vegetable, constitutes what I might designate as our basic arthritic's dinner, and roughly what you should stay with until you get results.

I suggest that you always prepare every other part of the meal first, and leave yourself absolutely free to concentrate on the fast, light touch with your fish.

SHELLFISH

Some of the easiest and most elegant ingredients of this diet are the shellfish. Lobster, crab, and shrimp are so good by themselves that they can be boiled and served with a bowl of safflower oil mayonnaise, a green salad, and a loaf of French bread. There are, of course, innumerable ways to serve these delicacies, some of which follow, but to my mind nothing surpasses the above.

CRACKED CRAB

This is the greatest feast; crab must be fresh to eat this way. It is cooked in boiling water and chilled, the claws are broken off the body and cracked, and the body is cut in pieces. Serve it on a bed of cracked ice to keep it very cold. A big bowl of safflower oil mayonnaise, and French bread, are called for, and you may complete the meal with a green salad.

FRESH CRAB

To my mind this is the best way to serve really fresh crab if you want a hot dish. Simply pile the crab in baking shells, pour melted margarine over it, and bake exactly 8 minutes in a hot oven (450 degrees).

BAKED CRAB IN SHELLS

2 cups fresh crab meat
1 cup safflower oil mayonnaise
½ teaspoon tarragon
Pinch dry hot mustard
About 1 teaspoon dry white wine (cheating again, but just enough to flavor)
Bread crumbs

Mix the crab meat, mayonnaise, tarragon, mustard, and wine; place in baking shells; top with the bread crumbs; dribble with melted margarine; and slide under broiler about 5 minutes or until nicely browned. This makes a nice rich first course.

CRAB PILAF

2 Dungeness crabs, cooked (this is the way they are almost always sold)
½ cup olive oil
1 onion, sliced
2 cups water
1½ cups clam juice
1½ teaspoons salt
1 cup uncooked rice
3 tablespoons chopped fresh mint leaves

Crack the crabs. Heat the oil in a heavy pan that has a tight lid, and sauté the onions till soft. Add the water, clam juice, and salt, and when boiling add the rice and mint. Cover, reduce the heat, and simmer slowly about 45 minutes. About 10 minutes before the rice is done, stir in the crab and remove the lid. In Greece this dish is cooked with tomatoes, but I found it to be very good cooked to our restrictions.

COLD BOILED LOBSTER

1½ to 2 pounds lobster
1 tablespoon chopped chives
¼ teaspoon each tarragon, parsley, and chervil
Pinch dry mustard
⅓ cup safflower oil mayonnaise
¼ cup olive oil

Boil the lobster, and either remove the meat from the shell and slice it or serve it in the shell. Mix all the other ingredients into a sauce, adding the oil last, gradually, to thin it.

STUFFING FOR BROILED LOBSTER

If you live on the West Coast you will use this for langouste or lobster tail.

1 cup bread crumbs
½ cup chopped clams
½ cup clam juice

Mix everything together and stuff into the cavity in the lobster shell. Or add to the bread crumbs: the coral (roe), the long, green liver, and about 4 tablespoons melted margarine.

CREAMED LOBSTER

1 cup lobster meat
2 tablespoons flour
3 tablespoons margarine
1½ cups clam juice
A few teaspoons of sherry!

Make a cream sauce from the roux of flour and margarine, gradually adding the clam juice. Heat the lobster in the sauce and add the sherry. You are cheating, but everyone has to cheat a tiny bit once in awhile, and this is *so* good.

LOBSTER AND CRAB PATTIES

1 cup lobster meat
1 cup crab meat
2 tablespoons margarine
1 tablespoon flour
½ cup water
½ cup safflower oil mayonnaise
1 teaspoon salt
Pinch nutmeg
1 cup cracker crumbs
6 tablespoons peanut oil

Remove all pieces of shell from the freshly cooked crab and lobster. Cut into nice bite-sized pieces. Make a roux of the margarine and flour, add the water to make a smooth, thick sauce, and remove from the fire. Stir in the mayonnaise, salt, and nutmeg; add the seafood. Cool at room temperature, chill in the refrigerator about 10 minutes, and shape into patties. Roll in the cracker crumbs, and fry in very hot peanut oil in a large skillet. Drain on absorbent paper.

ABALONE

Abalone is expensive and hard to come by unless you happen to live near the right kind of beach or have friends who do. We were lucky enough to have that combination some years ago and learned how to dive down and pry the shell from the rock with a tire iron. The cold Pacific is a great appetite whetter, and I can still taste that abalone cooked in the simple way described below (which I still think is best).

First, cut the abalone into slices about ⅜ inch thick and trim off all the dark that remains after cleaning. (If you bought them frozen, however, they're all ready to cook.) Pound them with a wooden mallet till they're limp—just enough to tenderize, not enough to tear the meat. Then simply drop them in sizzling margarine, lots of it, and sauté not more than a minute. I mean it! The secret in cooking abalone is that one minute!

BROILED ABALONE

1½ pounds abalone steaks
2 tablespoons margarine
2 tablespoons safflower oil mayonnaise
1 tablespoon minced parsley
Salt
Paprika

Cut the abalone about ½ inch thick and pound
well with a wooden mallet. Spread both sides with
margarine and place on the rack 2 inches below
the flame in a preheated hot broiler. After 5
minutes turn, spread with mayonnaise, and continue to broil 10 minutes. Serve garnished with
the minced parsley and sprinkled with a dash of
paprika.

OR: If the abalone is cut thin, pound with a
mallet and sauté rapidly in margarine 2 or 3
minutes each side.

SHRIMP

Shrimp happen to be one of the mainstays of my
daily sustenance. They're easily available, and in
their different forms and sizes can be prepared in
a great variety of ways. Our baby San Francisco
Bay shrimp are purchased all cooked and ready
to eat, and they make a perfect luncheon salad,
either with just lettuce and safflower oil mayonnaise, mixed with chopped celery and scallions, or
surrounded by cold vegetables with a garlic oil
dressing. Canned shrimp could be used the same
way.

Prawns are of the same family, though I find
people in different parts of the country differ

widely in what they consider a prawn. I am speaking of the very large raw shrimp, around 3 inches long before shelling. They're expensive and utterly delicious. They must be cooked delicately and briefly, and I don't like to spoil their flavor with too much seasoning of any kind. To remove the vein insert a pick into the back, about midway, and pull it out. If it breaks, repeat in a different spot.

BOILED SHRIMP

2 pounds shrimp (the regulation-size shrimp, not the tiny ones or the prawns)
1 teaspoon salt
3 tablespoons chopped parsley
2 cloves garlic
1 cup olive oil
1 tablespoon basil

Shell the shrimp and make a marinade of the other ingredients. Marinate the shrimp as long as possible, overnight perhaps, in a closely covered container in the refrigerator. To cook, place them in a shallow pan, pour the sauce over them, and broil under a brisk flame 5 to 8 minutes. Serve with the remaining marinade as sauce.

SHRIMP SPAGHETTI-TETRAZZINI

1 stick margarine
1 bunch scallions, thinly sliced and including a
    little of the tops
½ cup cold water
4 tablespoons cornstarch
2½ cups chicken broth
1 cup clam juice
½ teaspoon oregano
2 tablespoons corn oil
2 cloves garlic, crushed
½ pound mushrooms, sliced thin
½ pound spaghetti
2 pounds cooked medium shrimp
Salt

Melt half the margarine in a heavy pan. Add the
scallions and the water. Cook until the water has
boiled away and the scallions are soft. Stir in the
cornstarch (which has been mixed with a little
cold water) and stir for 1 minute; then add the
chicken broth, clam juice, and oregano. Stir constantly until it begins to boil; then set the pan
aside. Heat the remaining margarine in the oil
over high heat, and add the garlic and mushrooms. Toss and shake the pan until the mushrooms have browned—about 5 minutes.

Cook the spaghetti according to the directions
on the package; drain well. Mix all the ingredients
together in a large, shallow casserole and bake in
a 375-degree oven about 15 minutes, or until the
top is nicely browned.

INDONESIAN NASI GORENG

1 cup rice
1 large onion, chopped
1 clove garlic, crushed
½ pound small shrimp
Vegetable oil
Soy sauce

Boil the rice until done. Sauté the onions and garlic in the oil until golden; add the rice and shrimp. Heat through and add soy sauce to taste.

PRAWNS

I am very fond of prawns sautéed in a lot of margarine with their shells on. Devein them as described elsewhere, rinse and dry them, and sauté them in hot bubbling margarine just until they're quite pink. This is a messy way to eat them, since you must remove the heads and shell with your fingers, but it's delicious.

Another way is to shell them beforehand, finely chop some onion and green pepper, and sauté that first. Then when you add the prawns include some chopped basil and a tiny piece of crumbled bay leaf.

SHISH KEBAB

Scallops
Prawns
Green peppers, cut in hunks
Quartered onions
Large whole mushrooms

Use about two of each item per person. Marinate everything in olive oil and crushed garlic, bay leaf, tarragon, and oregano. Thread on skewers and barbecue or broil.

SAUTÉED OYSTERS ON TOAST

1 cup clam juice
1 dozen oysters, fresh or canned
French bread crumbs, salted

Dust the oysters with flour and let stand 15 minutes. Dip in clam juice and again let stand 15 minutes. Roll in crumbs. Sauté in generous amount of margarine until golden brown and crispy. Serve on toast made from a bread such as sprouted wheat. Sprinkle with freshly chopped parsley.

SCALLOPED OYSTERS

2 glass jars (about 10 ounces each) fresh oysters
¼ cup melted margarine
2 cups French bread crumbs
Salt

Drain the oysters; dry them carefully on paper towels. Dip each oyster in the melted margarine; then roll it in the bread crumbs till completely covered. Lay in a casserole, salting rather generously, and bake in a 350-degree oven 30 minutes.

CLAM SPAGHETTI

Two 8-ounce cans minced clams
16-ounce package thin spaghetti
1 stick margarine
3 tablespoons oil
1 clove garlic, crushed
1 onion, chopped
Salt

Sauté the onion and garlic in ½ stick margarine —do not brown. Add the juice from the clams; salt and simmer about 20 minutes. Add the clams just before serving; heat only long enough to make good and hot. Boil the spaghetti, meanwhile, in a large amount of well-salted water, making sure the strands are well separated. Cook *al dente*, in other words till firm to the bite, which should be 9 or 10 minutes. Drain off most of the water, but be sure to leave about ½ cup. This is the secret of good spaghetti. Add the other ½ stick of margarine and serve with the sauce.

Very often in winter we simply make the sauce, add a can of clam juice, and serve it as a soup with croutons made of cubed French bread fried in margarine.

EGGPLANT STUFFED WITH CLAMS

1 large eggplant
¼ cup minced onion
¼ cup margarine
8-ounce can minced clams
2 tablespoons minced parsley
½ teaspoon minced basil
1 cup soft French bread crumbs

Cut the top from the eggplant and scoop out the insides, being careful to leave enough shell to hold the filling. Chop the insides and cook in your French steamer until tender. In another pan sauté the onions in the margarine; add the cooked eggplant, clams, and herbs, and fill the eggplant shell. Sprinkle with some buttered crumbs and bake 30 minutes at 350 degrees. I think this is nice for a Sunday luncheon dish.

CLAM STEW

4 carrots
1 cup peas, fresh or frozen
6 small new potatoes
6 small white onions
4 stalks celery, scraped and sliced
12-ounce can clam juice
16-ounce can creamed corn
2 bay leaves
Basil, rosemary, thyme
Four 8-ounce cans minced or chopped clams
2 sticks margarine

Peel and cut up the vegetables; season and cover with clam juice, adding water as necessary to barely cover all the vegetables and seasonings. Simmer until tender; add the clams and margarine. Place in a casserole and cover the top with toasted rounds of French bread, cut with a cookie cutter.

CLAMS AND RICE, WEST COAST STYLE

    2 pounds steaming clams
    1 large bunch scallions, thinly sliced
    1 clove garlic, crushed
    ½ cup minced parsley
    ¼ cup finely chopped seeded green pepper
    3 tablespoons corn oil
    1 cup rice
    1½ cups water

Scrub the clams clean of all sand and wash them thoroughly in cold water several times. In a heavy pan such as a Dutch oven sauté the scallions, garlic, parsley, and pepper in the oil. When tender stir in the rice; then add the water and clams. Cover tightly and cook over medium heat till the rice is cooked—about 20 minutes. Taste for seasoning and serve in soup plates sprinkled with chopped parsley.

COQUILLES ST. JACQUES

1 pound scallops
2 cups water with small bay leaf, pinch thyme, few sprigs parsley
1 tablespoon chopped parsley
Bunch scallions, chopped
3 tablespoons margarine
Salt
2 tablespoons flour

Wash and drain the scallops. If large cut into pieces; if small leave whole. Simmer in the water till tender, about 5 or 6 minutes. Remove with a slotted spoon, set aside, and boil the water rapidly till reduced almost by half. If you're a garlic lover crush in 2 cloves garlic. Add the scallions and parsley; simmer in the liquid 10 minutes. Make a roux of the flour and margarine; gradually add the liquid; salt to taste. After you have a nice creamy sauce, stir in the scallops, place them in baking shells, top with bread crumbs, dot with margarine and slide under the broiler until nicely browned.

SAUTÉED SCALLOPS

Scallops are perhaps the most delicate of seafoods. They need only the quickest cooking and the simplest of seasonings.

1 pound scallops, either fresh or frozen and
   thawed
½ stick margarine
3 tablespoons water
1 tablespoon dry white wine
2 tablespoons minced parsley
Salt

Wash the scallops; dry carefully with paper
towels; flour very lightly. Melt the margarine and
add the scallops a few at a time, browning carefully on all sides. Immediately add the rest of the
ingredients and stir carefully with a wooden spoon
for a few minutes until they are heated through.

SCALLOPS IN BAKED POTATOES

2 to 3 pounds sea scallops
6 baking potatoes
½ cup margarine
2 teaspoons minced onion
Salt to taste (takes quite a lot)
Dash Worcestershire sauce
2 tablespoons cornstarch
2 cups cooked green peas

Cover the scallops with boiling water, add salt,
and cook very gently about 12 minutes. Drain and
save the broth. Poke the potatoes with a fork and
rub with margarine; bake 1 hour in a 400-degree
oven. Melt the ½ cup margarine, add the onion
and Worcestershire sauce, blend in the cornstarch (moistened with a little cold water), and

gradually add enough of the reserved broth to make a thick sauce. Salt to taste, add the scallops and peas, and serve over the baked potatoes.

FRIED SCALLOPS

Dip the scallops in clam juice, roll in yellow corn meal, and deep-fry in corn oil till golden brown. Serve with a safflower-oil mayonnaise sauce to which you've added diced cucumbers and minced scallions. Or you may arrange the scallops in a shallow pan and bake in a 425-degree oven about 10 minutes.

SCALLOPS PROVENÇAL

1½ pounds scallops
Flour, salted
6 tablespoons corn oil
2 cloves garlic, crushed
½ cup chopped parsley

Dust the scallops with the flour; heat the oil and add the garlic and scallops. Cook quickly, tossing and shaking the pan; salt to taste and add the chopped parsley.

SCALLOPS AMANDINE

1 pound scallops
Flour
⅓ cup margarine
2 tablespoons chopped parsley
½ cup slivered toasted almonds

Cut the scallops into bite-size pieces if large; dust with flour and brown in half the margarine till crisp and golden. Arrange on a heated serving dish. Melt the remaining margarine, add the almonds and parsley, and pour this over the scallops.

WHAT TO DO WITH SALMON

As I happen to consider salmon the king of fish, I like to devote some loving care to its preparation. If you are lucky enough—as we are here on the West Coast—to get it fresh, it just has to be the most delicious thing there is!

When you have a whole salmon, proceed in this manner: Of course it must be cleaned—something I always leave to someone else. However, I have the head left on, but I remove the gills myself. For some reason they have a bitter flavor. Rinse and dry the fish well, rub it all over with margarine, and wrap it securely in aluminum foil. Put it on a pan and bake it 10 minutes a pound in a 350-degree oven. Allow cooling time before serving, because it takes about 10 minutes for it to cool enough to make the skin slide off. When it is completely free of skin, slide it on a platter and

carefully cut the head off. Use your imagination
with cucumber and lemon slices, green and ripe
olives, and sprigs of parsley. Salmon is marvelous
either hot or cold, and when it's cold I also like to
serve safflower oil mayonnaise mixed with
chopped chives and parsley.

SALMON CHAUD-FROID

A really elegant way to present a salmon for a
Sunday lunch or even as a first course at your very
fanciest dinner is to glaze it with a chaud-froid.
In the first place, have your salmon as smooth as
possible. In this case you might refrigerate it before removing the skin because you're serving it
cold anyway. Now soften 2 tablespoons unflavored
gelatin in a cup of your chicken stock and dissolve
it over hot water. Blend this with 2 cups safflower
oil mayonnaise and watch it like a hawk. In about
15 minutes it will begin to thicken, and when it's
just setting—not stiff but not so thin that it will
run off the fish—pour it over the fish so that it
coats it evenly. Don't try to smooth out any places
with a knife; just pour the coating on and leave it
alone. Refrigerate the fish and then decorate it
suitably: a ripe olive slice for an eye, cucumber
slices for the scales, parsley for the tail, etc. Of
course, any whole fish can be prepared this way
but it's best for larger fish, which are easier to
bone when serving.

SALMON STEAKS WITH BUTTER SAUCE

2 pounds salmon steaks (4 steaks if small, 2 if large)
1 tablespoon olive oil
2 tablespoons margarine
Salt
4 shallots, minced
4 tablespoons water
1½ sticks margarine, chilled and cut into small pieces

Marinate the fish in the olive oil 30 minutes, turning once. Broil 7 minutes on each side, and arrange on a hot serving dish. Keep warm. Sauté the shallots very gently in 1 tablespoon margarine until soft; add the water and reduce gently until 2 tablespoons of liquid remain. Remove the pan from the burner and beat in 2 pieces of the chilled margarine with a wire whisk. Return the pan to the heat and beat in the rest of the margarine piece by piece. Serve immediately.

I had what I think was the most perfectly cooked piece of salmon I have yet to taste at the Cypress Point Club at Pebble Beach. It was a fillet —the part toward the tail (the best)—and it had been brushed with a little oil and broiled. They'd dusted a little paprika on it so that it browned with a lovely crisp crust; it hadn't been turned, but their secret, as they told me, was that they'd turned off the broiler and left it there for a while after it browned.

SALMON MOUSSE

1½ tablespoons unflavored gelatin
½ cup cold water
2 cups cooked, flaked salmon
3 teaspoons grated onion
2 tablespoons capers
1 tablespoon soy sauce
1 cup safflower oil mayonnaise
Merest dash tabasco
Salt to taste

Soften the gelatin in the water and heat gently until dissolved; set aside to cool. Combine the other ingredients, fold in the cooled gelatin, and put in a 4-cup fish mold. This is nice served with thinly sliced cucumbers mixed with safflower oil mayonnaise and a little dill weed.

FILLET OF SOLE

This is probably the most available and adaptable fish for general use. It's not too expensive and almost all markets have it in either fresh or frozen form. The varieties of ways to serve it are practically infinite; furthermore, there are quite a few different kinds of sole. In the first place, the real sole is a European fish, but we call our flounder, lemon sole, gray sole, dab, and petrale all by the general name of sole. Petrale and gray sole are perhaps the best, since they hold together in cooking better than lemon sole or flounder, but all are good.

I have a heavy aluminum shallow baking dish that is perfect for the cooking of sole. It's not quite 2 inches deep, and is long and narrow to accommodate the shape of the fillet.

SOLE AMANDINE

- ½ cup slivered almonds
- 2 tablespoons sliced shallots
- 6 tablespoons margarine
- ½ cup blanched almonds pulverized in the blender
- 1½ pounds sole fillets
- ½ cup clam juice
- 1 tablespoon cornstarch

Sauté the shallots for just a few minutes in a little of the margarine, stir in the almonds with the rest of the margarine, and add salt to taste. Smooth this paste on one side of each fillet and lay the fillets in a margarined shallow fish casserole. Pour the clam juice around them (and if you're quite well now, add a little white wine). Bake till the fish separates easily with a fork, about 20 minutes, in a 350-degree oven. Remove the fish from the liquid, boil the liquid down to about a cup, and blend in the cornstarch. When this is thickened add the slivered almonds, pour it over the fillets, and serve.

SOLE BONNE FEMME

¼ pound fresh mushrooms, chopped
1 tablespoon minced shallot
3 tablespoons parsley
1½ pounds sole fillets
1 cup court bouillon (see page 59)

Mix the mushrooms, shallot, and parsley, and spread on the bottom of the margarined shallow casserole or pan. Salt the fillets, arrange them on the mushrooms, and pour the court bouillon over all. Cook about 20 minutes in a 350-degree oven, remove the fillets (keep them warm), and reduce the sauce to about a cup. Add 2 tablespoons margarine and pour over the sole. Garnish with parsley sprigs and serve.

SOLE MEUNIÈRE

6 sole fillets
Flour
6 tablespoons margarine
3 tablespoons corn oil
Chopped parsley

Dredge the fillets lightly in flour; season with salt. Melt the margarine with the oil in a heavy skillet and sauté the fillets rather quickly, turning once. When nicely brown remove the fish to a hot serving platter, add 3 more tablespoons margarine and the chopped parsley to the pan, and pour everything in the pan over the fish.

BROILED FILLETS OF SOLE

4 tablespoons olive oil
3 shallots, minced
1 clove garlic, crushed
1 teaspoon basil
1 teaspoon salt
2 tablespoons chopped parsley
6 sole fillets, rather larger, firmer ones

Sauté the shallots and the garlic in the oil and add the seasonings. Simmer about 5 minutes. Brush the fillets with oil and place on the broiler rack. Broil 5 minutes, turn, pour the sauce over them, and continue broiling another 4 or 5 minutes until the fish is done.

BROILED SOLE WITH HERBS

6 sole fillets
1½ teaspoons salt
1 stick margarine
2 tablespoons chopped chives
2 tablespoons chopped parsley
1 teaspoon tarragon

Place the fillets on an oiled broiling rack and spread with the mixture of the other ingredients. Broil about 4 minutes on each side.

SOLE IN BREAD CRUMBS

6 sole fillets
1 cup French bread crumbs
1 teaspoon salt
1 tablespoon chopped parsley
1 tablespoon fresh dill or tarragon (1 teaspoon
  if dried)
1 cup clam juice
Flour
6 tablespoons margarine
3 tablespoons safflower or corn oil

Mix the crumbs, herbs, and salt. Dip the fillets in
the clam juice, roll lightly in the flour, dip in the
clam juice again, and then roll in the crumbs.
Sauté till browned (about 7 minutes) in the oil
and margarine.

FILLETS OF SOLE NIÇOISE

2 cloves garlic, crushed
1 onion, chopped fine
1 teaspoon salt
1 teaspoon rosemary
About 20 pitted large black olives
18 anchovies
2 tablespoons chopped parsley
½ teaspoon summer savory
7 tablespoons margarine
6 good-sized sole fillets
12-ounce bottle of clam juice

Combine the clam juice, 1 clove garlic, the onion, the salt, ½ teaspoon rosemary, and 4 tablespoons margarine in a pan and bring to a boil. Reduce heat and simmer 15 minutes. Add 8 of the olives and reduce heat to very low while preparing the fish. Chop the anchovies and remaining olives and add the remaining garlic clove. Blend into this mixture the remaining margarine and rosemary, the parsley, and the summer savory. Spread each fillet with some of the mixture; roll it up and secure it with toothpicks. Place the fish in a shallow pan just large enough to accommodate them, and pour over them the clam juice sauce. Poach the fillets till done by the fork test, about 15 minutes. Remove to an ovenproof serving dish, sprinkle with chopped parsley, and run under the broiler for just a minute.

COLD POACHED FILLET OF SOLE

Poach the desired number of fillets in court bouillon (see page 59) to cover generously. Cool, then refrigerate. These can be served with several types of safflower oil mayonnaise: one mixed with grated cucumber and dill, or one mixed with herbs such as tarragon and greens such as chopped spinach, watercress, and parsley.

SOLE FILLETS IN BAKED POTATO

4 or 5 oval-shaped potatoes
½ cup small shrimp
3 tablespoons margarine
Salt to taste
Handful chopped parsley
1½ cups cream sauce (made of 2 tablespoons flour, 2 tablespoons margarine, and the poaching stock)
4 or 5 sole fillets
½ bay leaf
1 slice onion

Bake the potatoes in a 350-degree oven 1 hour or till soft. Toss the shrimp in 1 tablespoon margarine; season with the salt and parsley. Fold the sole over and poach in just enough water to cover, adding the bay leaf and onion. Now slice the top off each potato and scoop out some of the inside. Put the shrimp in each, and add a fillet. Add the sauce and replace the top of the potato.

FILLET OF SOLE WITH SHRIMP SAUCE

4 portion-sized sole fillets
½ pound small shrimp, or the canned equivalent
1 carrot
1 onion
1 celery stalk
1 bay leaf
1 clove
A little thyme
1 tablespoon flour
2 tablespoons margarine
About 1½ cups clam juice

Bring to a boil in a poaching pan about 2 inches
water with the vegetables, herbs, and spices. Add
salt, reduce heat, and poach the sole 5 or 6 minutes until it flakes with a fork. Make a roux of the
flour and margarine, thin with the clam juice, add
the shrimp, and mask the fish. Sprinkle with a
little paprika and slide under the broiler to brown
nicely.

FILLET OF POMPANO

Boneless fillet of pompano (or other firm fillet)
2 teaspoons finely grated fresh coconut
1 stick margarine
3 tablespoons slivered browned almonds

Poach the fillet slowly in ½ inch water in a
covered pan, for 5 minutes. Place under the
broiler covered with the fresh coconut; broil till

the fish flakes with a fork. Serve with a sauce made of melted margarine into which has been beaten some of the poaching stock and the browned almonds and salt to taste.

FROG'S LEGS PROVENÇAL

8 frog's legs
5 tablespoons margarine
4 cloves garlic, crushed
2 tablespoons fresh tarragon, chives, and parsley, finely chopped

Wash the frog's legs; dry and dust lightly with salted flour. Melt the margarine and add the garlic. Cook 1 minute; then add the frog's legs and sauté till golden brown on both sides. Add the herbs, taste for seasoning, and cook just 1 minute more, or until a fork test shows they are done.

STUFFED TURBOT

4 flat pieces of turbot
½ pound crab meat
¼ cup safflower oil mayonnaise
1 teaspoon Grey Poupon mustard
1 tablespoon soy sauce

Mix the crab with the condiments and arrange on the pieces of turbot. Roll up the pieces and fasten with toothpicks. Place them in a pan in which they will fit rather snugly and sprinkle lightly with paprika to brown. Bake in a 350-degree oven 20 minutes.

TUNA LOAF

3 slices French bread, crusts cut off (whole grain bread is good too)
2 family-sized cans white chunky tuna (albacore)
1 small grated onion
Salt
½ teaspoon thyme

Soak the bread in a cup of water 30 minutes or so. Add the onion and seasonings, stir well, and add the tuna. Mix, place in a loaf pan, and press into loaf shape. It will stick together if you have enough bread in it and press it firmly enough. Bake in a 350-degree oven 30 minutes or until brown and crisp on top.

EGGPLANT AND TUNA

Parboil the eggplant; split it and scoop out the pulp. Combine the pulp with a 7-ounce can of white tuna (albacore) and 2 tablespoons corn oil. Season with onion salt and chopped basil. Heat through in the oven.

TUNA CASSEROLE

½ stick margarine
1 smallish minced onion
2 tablespoons flour
Two 7-ounce cans white tuna (albacore)
1½ cups clam juice

Melt the margarine and sauté the onion. Gradually work in the flour to make a smooth mixture; add the clam juice gradually and stir till thick. Pour this over the tuna in a shallow casserole and top with French bread crumbs. Bake in a 350-degree oven 20 minutes.

TUNABURGERS

7-ounce can white chunky tuna (albacore)
½ cup safflower oil mayonnaise
¼ cup bread crumbs
2 tablespoons finely chopped onions
2 tablespoons finely chopped green pepper
½ teaspoon oregano
Garlic salt

Mix well and press into patties. They should hold together, but if you have trouble, here's the place for the soybean-flour egg yolk mentioned on page 32. Grill over charcoal, about 4 minutes on each side, putting aluminum foil under them if necessary to keep them from falling through the grill.

FISH STEW PROVENÇAL

5 medium potatoes, sliced
1 onion, sliced
2 cloves garlic, crushed
Salt
1 bay leaf
1 celery stalk, broken in half
2 large sprigs parsley
Pinch fennel seeds
⅓ cup olive oil
2 pounds fresh white-fleshed fish fillets, cut into large bite-sized pieces (you can have several varieties of fish, whatever you choose)

Arrange the fillets in a large, heavy casserole. Cover them with the potatoes; add the onion and garlic. Add the seasonings and herbs, pour the olive oil over them, and cover everything with boiling water. Bring to a boil and simmer gently about 20 minutes or until the vegetables are tender. Remove the bay leaf, celery, and parsley before serving in large soup plates.

FILLET OF HADDOCK WITH CRAB SAUCE

About 1½ pounds haddock fillets
½ stick margarine
2 tablespoons onion juice
¼ teaspoon salt

Melt the butter; add the seasonings. Dip the fish in the mixture, flour very lightly, place in a shallow pan, and bake at 450 degrees 20 minutes.

SAUCE

2 tablespoons margarine
¾ cup crab meat
2 tablespoons cornstarch, mixed with a litt
   cold water
¼ teaspoon salt
1 cup clam juice
A suspicion of sherry

Sauté the crab meat in the margarine in a covere
pan 5 minutes. Mix the dry ingredients and ad
them, stirring constantly. Add the clam juice anc
just at the last minute, the dash of sherry.

SCALLOPED FISH

6 pieces flounder or any other boned fish
4 large onions
1 pound fresh mushrooms
1½ cups French bread crumbs
¾ cup margarine

Chop the onions and mushrooms, sauté in th
margarine, add the crumbs to make a thick paste
and season with salt. In a margarined casserol
place a layer of the crumb mixture alternatel
with a layer of fish, topping with the crumb mix
ture. Bake in a 350-degree oven till the fish flake
with a fork, about 45 minutes to an hour.

STUFFED LAKE TROUT

Lake trout (weighing between 3 and 5 pounds)
2 cups French bread crumbs, fresh
1 small minced onion
1 tablespoon chopped parsley
Large pinch thyme
Pinch nutmeg
Salt
3 tablespoons clam juice

Mix all the seasonings with the bread crumbs, add the clam juice, and mix well. Stuff the trout lightly with this mixture, place in an oiled baking dish, and if you have dressing left place it over the fish. Bake in a 375-degree oven about 40 minutes. Garnish with parsley and fresh mint.

FRESHWATER FISH EN PAPILLOTTE

Take a trout, or other small freshwater fish (cleaned, of course), and after wiping with a damp cloth salt it inside and out. Spread margarine over a large piece of wax paper and wrap the fish securely, tying it if necessary. A little fresh chopped mint may be sprinkled on the fish before wrapping. Place in a shallow baking dish and bake in a 400-degree oven about 50 minutes. The time will vary according to the size of the fish. Fifty minutes is right for one weighing about 5 pounds. Serve directly from the paper.

RAINBOW TROUT

These little wonders are best cooked in corn meal in the time-honored way of the flycaster. If you've been lucky enough to catch them yourself, they'l taste wonderful no matter what you do to them but they are available frozen in some markets, and properly defrosted first are quite acceptable. Rub them with salt, roll them in yellow corn meal, and sauté in a generous amount of margarine, allow-ing about 10 minutes to the first side and 5 to the second.

STEAMED FRESHWATER FISH

Use rock bass, lake trout, or whitefish, which have been wiped with a damp cloth and in which you have placed a clove of garlic and a bay leaf. Place the fish in a wire basket over a pan of water, cover the pan, and steam 15 minutes. Serve with this sauce: Cook together 2 tablespoons cornstarch (moistened with water) and 2 tablespoons mar-garine to make a roux and gradually add 1½ cups clam juice and ¼ cup soy sauce.

STRIPED BASS

Striped bass are available from both the Atlantic and Pacific waters; they are different in color but are essentially the same fish. Ask the fishmarket to bone them for you—it makes for much pleasanter eating.

HERB-STUFFED BASS

1 whole striped bass, about 4 pounds
4 cups French bread crumbs, dry
1 large onion, minced
2 stalks celery, minced
1 teaspoon salt
¼ teaspoon thyme
Pinch each tarragon and rosemary
6 tablespoons margarine

Sauté the onion and celery in the margarine; add to bread crumbs with the rest of the seasonings. Stuff the fish loosely and fasten with toothpicks or skewers; rub with margarine and place in an oiled pan. Bake 40 minutes in a 350-degree oven.

BASS WITH MINT AND GARLIC

1 whole striped bass, about 4 pounds
½ cup olive oil
½ cup French bread crumbs, dry
1 tablespoon minced parsley
1 teaspoon salt
6 sprigs fresh mint
2 cloves garlic, crushed
1 teaspoon chopped fresh basil, or pinch of dry
½ cup clam juice

Mix the crumbs with the parsley, salt, and basil; add 2 tablespoons oil, the garlic, and the mint sprigs. Stuff the fish, securing with skewers, and place in a margarined baking dish. Pour the re-

maining oil over the fish and bake in a 350-de
gree oven 40 minutes. Baste frequently with th
pan drippings.

STUFFED STRIPED BASS, GREEK STYLE

I love the food in Greece—the fish is wonderful
and I used to wonder why I felt so marvelou
there. It's understandable when you realize tha
the Greeks use the most basic ingredients, such a:
olive oil, onions, celery, nuts, and simple herbs.

1 whole striped bass, 3 or 4 pounds
½ cup olive oil
1 tablespoon oregano
2 tablespoons chopped parsley
Stuffing
Melted margarine
Salt

Have the fishman clean the bass, leaving on the
tail. Salt the inside of the fish and fill with the
stuffing described below (any remaining stuffing
may be cooked in a covered casserole). Secure the
fish with skewers and string, brush it with melted
margarine, and place it in a baking pan. Combine
the oil, parsley, and oregano and pour this over
the fish. Bake 1 hour at 375 degrees. Serve garnished with Greek olives.

STUFFING FOR BASS

2 cups rice
4½ cups clam juice
3 tablespoons chopped parsley
1 cup chopped onions
1 cup chopped celery
¼ pound margarine
½ cup pine nuts
Salt

Steam the rice in 4 cups clam juice 20 minutes. Sauté the onions, parsley, and celery in the margarine until golden; add the rice and pine nuts, salt to taste, and add the remaining ½ cup clam juice.

HADDOCK OR COD WITH NUTS

3 pounds haddock or cod steaks
½ cup olive oil
2 onions, chopped
2 tablespoons chopped parsley
½ cup water
1 tablespoon each walnuts, almonds, and hazel nuts, chopped in blender
2 tablespoons French bread crumbs
1 cup court bouillon (see page 59)

Sauté the onions and parsley in the oil over a low flame. Add the fish steaks and water; simmer 15 minutes. In a separate pan brown the nuts, stirring constantly; add the bread crumbs and stir until brown. Add the fish stock, and bring to a boil while continuing to stir. Pour the sauce over the fish, and serve with toasted French bread.

COD OR BASS WITH EGGPLANT

2 pounds cod or bass fillets
1 eggplant
1 stick margarine

Slice the eggplant, salt each slice, and allow it to stand under a weight such as a heavy iron skillet for an hour. Drain away the resulting water. Sauté the fish and eggplant together in the margarine about 10 minutes. Serve with this Greek sauce:

SAUCE

4 large cloves garlic, crushed
1 teaspoon salt
1 cup olive oil
½ cup toasted almonds

COD OR SEA BASS WITH PINE NUTS

1½ pounds boned or filleted fish
1 cup chopped leeks
½ cup finely chopped onion
2 tablespoons margarine
2 tablespoons olive oil
1 large clove garlic, crushed
¼ teaspoon thyme
½ teaspoon sage
Salt
12-ounce bottle of clam juice
4 tablespoons chopped parsley

Sauté the leeks and onion in the oil and margarine; add the garlic and seasonings. Add the clam juice and simmer uncovered about 30 minutes; add the parsley. Meanwhile, the fish has been quickly sautéed in oil until golden brown on both sides. Now arrange the fish in an oiled baking dish, pour the sauce over it, and sprinkle with pine nuts; bake 25 minutes in a 350-degree oven.

Polenta is good with this very Italian dish. Simply add 1 cup corn meal slowly to 4 cups boiling water; boil, stirring, 5 minutes; add 4 tablespoons margarine; and bake in a 350-degree oven until set, about 50 minutes.

ITALIAN FISH CASSEROLE

½ cup almonds
2 carrots
Stalk celery
¼ pound mushrooms
2 medium onions
1½ pounds codfish fillets
Salt and margarine

Chop all the vegetables fine; mix together. Line a casserole with half the vegetables and lay the fish fillets on them. Add salt and cover with the remaining vegetables. Sprinkle with the chopped almonds, and moisten with about 1 cup clam juice. Cover and bake 30 minutes in a 350-degree oven, removing the cover the last 10 minutes. Serve with margarined spaghetti or noodles.

CODFISH CAKES WITH SKORDALIA

1 pound packaged salt codfish
1 bay leaf
1 onion, quartered
2 cups mashed potatoes
2 scallions, chopped fine
2 tablespoons finely chopped parsley
2 tablespoons olive oil
3 tablespoons margarine

Prepare the codfish according to the directions on the box, repeating the soakings and boilings at least four times. The last time add the bay leaf and onion to the pot and boil slowly 20 minutes. Drain, and remove the bay leaf and onion. If the cod is still salty boil again with cold water; drain. Place the fish in a collander; mash and squeeze it with your hands until all the water is removed and it is well mashed. Add the mashed potatoes, scallions, and parsley; knead and shape the mixture into patties on a floured board. Dust them with flour and sauté in margarine and oil until golden brown. Serve with the following sauce.

SKORDALIA

6 cloves garlic, crushed
2 cups mashed potatoes
½ teaspoon salt
1 cup olive oil

Purée the garlic, potatoes, and salt in the blender till smooth; then slowly pour in the olive oil. If too thick, thin with a little water. Chill before serving.

COD IN CASSEROLE

2 pounds packaged salt codfish
4 large potatoes, boiled and sliced
3 tablespoons minced parsley
1 teaspoon oregano

Prepare the codfish as in the recipe for codfish cakes, but in this the codfish should be flaked instead of mashed. Place a layer of codfish flakes in an oiled casserole, add a layer of sliced potatoes, dot with margarine, top with a layer of codfish, and sprinkle with oregano and parsley. Cover with a white sauce made of 3 tablespoons flour, ¼ cup margarine, and 2 cups clam juice to which you have added 2 cloves crushed garlic. Bake in a 300-degree oven 1 hour.

SHAD ROE

I really think shad roe is my all-time favorite in the delicacy department. Whenever I feel like going on a binge, I have shad roe—fresh when it's available, which is practically never, or canned. Either way it's shamefully expensive. The following preparation is for fresh shad roe (the canned I simply slide carefully into a little bubbling margarine and sauté gently till it's heated through, sometimes adding a little garlic).

2 pairs shad roe
1 bay leaf
2 tablespoons margarine
1 clove garlic, crushed
1 teaspoon minced parsley

Place the shad roe in a pan and barely cover with water; add the bay leaf. Cook over a very low flame until the water comes to a boil; the gradual heating toughens the skin, hopefully keeping all the little precious eggs inside. Remove the shad roe from the water; drain and dry very carefully. Sauté in the margarine with the garlic and parsley until golden brown. When serving, pour the margarine remaining in the pan over the shad roe.

8

Chicken

As MENTIONED earlier, the white meat of chicken breasts may be added as an occasional change. I waited over a year before I tried it, but this is up to the individual's common sense. I've never noticed any ill effect from it, and its very versatility makes it a wonderful addition to our menus.

CHICKEN STEW

4 chicken breasts
1½ cups water
½ stick margarine
2 tablespoons flour
Pinch each thyme and rosemary
12 small boiling onions, peeled
½ pound fresh mushrooms

Sprinkle the chicken generously with salt and brown in the margarine, using a heavy skillet or

Dutch oven. Remove the chicken from the pan
and blend the flour and herbs in the remaining
margarine. When smooth, gradually stir in the
water, and when the mixture comes to a boil, add
the chicken and onions. Simmer 20 minutes; add
the mushrooms; simmer 10 minutes or until
everything is done.

BREAST OF CHICKEN WITH WILD RICE
(for 1 person)

1 chicken breast
1 small onion
1 carrot
1 stalk tender celery
Sliver of garlic
1 large mushroom, chopped
1 tablespoon cornstarch
1 tablespoon margarine
1 cup chicken broth
½ cup wild rice

In a small pan make a cream sauce of the margarine, cornstarch, and broth. Bone and skin the
chicken breast, season with salt, and place in a
heavy margarined skillet. Add the onion, carrot,
celery, garlic, mushroom, and cream sauce. Cover
the pan and simmer slowly until the breast is
done. In the meantime, soak and wash ½ cup
wild rice; boil 20 minutes and keep warm over
steam till the chicken is ready. At the last minute
a whisper of sherry is a nice addition to the
chicken before serving it over the mound of wild
rice.

BAKED CHICKEN WITH HERBS

6 chicken breasts
5 tablespoons olive oil
½ teaspoon each thyme, basil, and marjoram
1 tablespoon fresh cut chives
Flour and salt
1 tablespoon minced parsley

Wipe the breasts with a damp cloth. Place in a bowl and pour 3 tablespoons oil over them; sprinkle with the mixed herbs and chives. Cover and let stand in the refrigerator 3 or 4 hours. Lift the chicken from the marinade, dust lightly with flour, and brown 15 minutes in 2 tablespoons oil. Arrange the breasts in a large, shallow casserole in one layer; sprinkle lightly with salt. Mix the marinade remaining in the bowl with 1 cup water; add the parsley to it and pour this over the chicken. Cover and bake in a 375-degree oven 30 minutes. Uncover periodically to see if the chicken is done; baste frequently with the marinade in the casserole.

CHICKEN MARENGO

6 chicken breasts
½ cup flour
1 teaspoon tarragon
1 teaspoon salt
¼ cup olive oil
½ stick margarine
1½ cups water
2 cloves garlic, crushed
¼ pound mushrooms, thinly sliced

Shake the chicken in a paper bag with the flour, salt, and tarragon. Save the remaining flour. Heat the oil and margarine in a heavy skillet and brown the chicken carefully. Transfer to a heavy casserole. Stir the remaining flour into the oil and margarine left in the skillet and when a smooth paste add the water and stir until thickened and smooth. Pour this sauce over the chicken, add the garlic and mushrooms, and bake 30 minutes in a 350-degree oven. Sprinkle with minced parsley before serving.

CHICKEN BREASTS WITH GARLIC

    4 large chicken breasts
    2 heads fresh garlic (peeled by slapping with
      the flat side of a big knife)
    ½ cup olive oil
    3 stalks celery, sliced thin
    4 sprigs parsley
    ½ teaspoon tarragon
    1 teaspoon salt
    Pinch nutmeg

Pour the oil into a heavy casserole with a tight-fitting lid. Turn the breasts over in the oil; add the peeled garlic cloves, celery, and parsley; sprinkle the seasonings over this and mix everything together well. Put foil over the top of the casserole, put on the tight lid, and then put more heavy foil over the lid. You want to have the chicken sealed as completely as possible during the entire cooking time. Cook 1½ hours in a 375-degree oven, and serve with toasted French bread to eat with the soft garlic.

GREEK-STYLE CHICKEN

6 chicken breasts
3 cups water
1 teaspoon garlic salt
1 onion, sliced
4 stalks celery, sliced
1 bay leaf
1 tablespoon minced parsley
Pinch poultry seasoning
1 tablespoon flour
2 teaspoons cornstarch
4 tablespoons cold water

Remove the skin from the chicken breasts; place them in a covered pot with the 3 cups water, seasonings, vegetables, and parsley. Simmer until tender, about a half-hour. Remove the chicken to a serving dish and keep it warm. Make a paste of the flour, cornstarch, and cold water and stir it into the simmering broth. When thickened, pour it over the chicken.

9

Vegetables

VEGETABLES ARE your principal source of enzymes, vitamins, and minerals. If you're not particularly turned on by vegetables, I suggest you experiment until you find ones you like; vegetables are an absolutely essential element of this diet. Really, they *can* be interesting!

Many vegetables also contain protein—cabbage, carrots, celery, corn, green peppers, and all the bean family. The vital enzymes, which as I explained earlier do not function properly unless the vegetables are raw, are abundant in the unrefined vegetable oils and the leafy green vegetables, as well as in garlic and onions . . . and again, cabbage. Potatoes contain vitamin B-1 (thiamine), vitamin B-2 (riboflavin), niacin, vitamin C, and iron. You'd do well to include them often in your menu, baked or boiled.

Broccoli, asparagus, carrots, corn, lettuce, peas, spinach, string beans, parsley, and watercress are some of the vegetables rich in vitamin A. The vegetables having the B vitamins are dried peas and beans, lentils, beets, cabbage, corn, broccoli, and potatoes. (Peanuts, soybeans, sunflower seeds, brewer's yeast, and wheat germ are also rich in B.) Our best sources of vitamin C are potatoes, green peppers, brussels sprouts, and other green vegetables.

In addition to the vitamins supplied by vegetables there are all the minerals: calcium, chlorine, copper, iodine, iron, magnesium, phosphorus, potassium, silicon, sulfur, and zinc.

All the foregoing should convince you that vegetables are very important and not to be slighted. It happens that corn, cabbage, and baked potatoes are the vegetables my husband and I mutually enjoy the most, so they appear quite regularly on our table. However, I've gradually become quite addicted to all vegetables and find myself craving a raw carrot when in the old days it would have been a chocolate cream. I even find them quite beautiful to look at when properly prepared and presented; I like to see vegetables such as carrots and green beans cooked whole, particularly when young and attractive. And a platter of skillfully arranged raw vegetables can become a work of art.

COOKING VEGETABLES

I find a French vegetable steamer indispensable. The vegetables stay firm and crisp and retain their vitamins and minerals. I like carrots, green beans, cauliflower, or peas slightly undercooked and served with a little olive oil in which I've crushed a clove of garlic. Salt is pretty much the only seasoning vegetables need, but occasionally I add a little marjoram and thyme to green beans, a little dill to cucumbers, or a little basil to most anything.

BAKED VEGETABLES

When you want to have a vegetable that will be ready at the last minute with no further attention needed, bake it.

Scrape baby carrots and place them in a heavy skillet with a stick of margarine and 2 crushed garlic cloves; cover tightly. Bake in a 350-degree oven 1 hour.

You can do the same thing with beets.

Soak a cauliflower 1 hour in salt water. Separate into flowerettes and place in a margarined casserole. Sprinkle with a little water and dot with ½ stick margarine (or more, depending on the size of the cauliflower). Cover and bake in a *very* slow oven 3½ hours.

ARTICHOKES

Cut the stem off at the base of 4 artichokes; pull off any tough outer leaves; cut about an inch from the top; and clip each leaf to remove its sharp thorny tip. Stand the artichokes in a large kettle and add about 1½ inches water. Add 1 tablespoon olive oil, 2 cloves, 1 bay leaf, and a liberal amount of garlic salt. Cover tightly and steam till one of

the large leaves pulls off easily. Drain upside
down and serve with safflower oil mayonnaise
mixed with a little soy sauce.

ASPARAGUS WITH BASIL

    1 cup soft French bread crumbs
    3 pounds asparagus
    1 small onion, minced
    1 stick margarine
    2 teaspoons chopped basil
    1 teaspoon salt

Cook the asparagus, uncovered, 5 minutes in a
skillet with about ½ inch water; cover and continue cooking until the tough part of the stalk is
tender. In a separate pan heat the margarine and
brown the crumbs, onion, and basil. I always have
an old Turkish towel handy for drying asparagus;
simply lay it on the towel and fold the towel over
to keep it warm till you want it. Anything served
over it, such as this crumb mixture, is absorbed
into the stalk and twice as tasty.

CURRIED GREEN BEANS

    1 package (10-12 ounces) frozen whole green
      beans
    ⅓ cup safflower oil mayonnaise
    2 tablespoons minced onion
    ¼ teaspoon salt
    Small pinch curry powder

Cook the beans as directed on the package. Mix the remaining ingredients and stir into the well-drained beans; heat thoroughly, but not enough to let the mayonnaise separate. Again I must say that you don't add spices such as this pinch of curry powder until you've been feeling really well for quite a long time. Your body will be able to handle these after it's in a proper balance, but only in small quantities.

LIMA BEANS WITH SAGE

1 package (10-12 ounces) frozen baby lima beans
½ stick margarine
1 teaspoon sage
Garlic salt

Cook the beans according to the directions on the package, adding the sage to the water. When done, drain, not disturbing whatever sage wants to adhere to the beans; add the margarine and salt.

BRUSSELS SPROUTS WITH CHESTNUTS

Make a cross on 8 chestnuts. Boil them 45 minutes in salted water; cool and peel. Boil 1 pound brussels sprouts; mix with the chestnuts; add margarine, salt, and a dash of nutmeg.

BRAISED CELERY WITH MUSHROOM SAUCE

Cut fresh young celery in uniformly sized stalks. Place in a pan, cover with water, and add ½ cup soy sauce. Braise slowly, covered, until tender. Meanwhile mince some very fresh mushrooms and sauté in a saucepan about 10 minutes, stirring. Add salt, a pinch of nutmeg, and a generous piece of margarine; cook over low heat, stirring often. Drain the celery and cover it with the mushrooms.

CABBAGE

Cut a tender new head of cabbage into eighths or quarters, depending on the size. Cook in a French steamer till it pierces with a fork—not very long. Pour over it melted margarine, in which you have crushed a few dill seeds.

TENNESSEE CABBAGE

Place 3 tablespoons margarine in an iron skillet and brown slightly. Add 1 small head shredded cabbage and stir well. Cover tightly and simmer 5 minutes. Stir again, cover, and simmer 5 minutes longer. Add ½ teaspoon salt and ½ cup water in which you have dissolved 1 tablespoon cornstarch; stir well. Cover and simmer 3 or 4 minutes. Time is very important, since the cabbage may be spoiled by overcooking. Serve very hot.

CORN COOKERY

My husband and I absolutely adore corn, and it's a wonderful food. (Look at the peoples of the world who've lived well on maize . . . think of the white teeth of the Mexicans.) Here in California we're fortunate enough to be able to get it almost all year round, but the frozen corn, both on the cob and cut off, is very good. (Of course you will carefully read your labels so as to buy frozen vegetables to which NOTHING has been added.)

I've never been able to improve on the old-fashioned way of starting the corn on the cob in cold water, bringing it to a boil, and taking it off after 3 minutes. Another great favorite of mine, actually from my childhood, is corn cut off and lightly sautéed with slivered green pepper.

SAUTÉED CUCUMBERS

Peel the cucumbers, cut in strips, and remove the seeds. Sauté in margarine and a little salt 10 minutes. Blend in 1 teaspoon flour and add finely chopped parsley.

EGGPLANT CASSEROLE

    1 large eggplant
    4 boiling onions
    ½ cup flour
    ½ stick margarine
    Bread crumbs

Peel the eggplant and boil it in salted water; drain it thoroughly and mash it lightly. Sauté the onions in 1 heaping tablespoon margarine until soft. Make a roux of flour and margarine, mix all the ingredients together and salt generously to taste. Cover with crumbs, dot with margarine, and bake 20 minutes in a 350-degree oven.

FRIED EGGPLANT

Slice the eggplant, soak in cold water 1 hour, drain with a weight on top, and dry carefully. Dust with flour which has been seasoned with a little basil and garlic salt, and fry in a mixture of ½ cup olive oil and ½ cup margarine until golden brown.

BRAISED ENDIVES

    8 Belgian endives
    2 tablespoons melted margarine
    Salt

Arrange the endives in an oiled casserole. Pour on the margarine and salt, and add about ¼ cup water. Cover tightly and bake in a 350-degree oven 45 minutes, or until the endives are tender.

GREEN PEPPERS

3 tablespoons olive oil
2 onions, sliced thin
2 green peppers, seeded and cut in strips
1 clove garlic, crushed
1 tablespoon chopped fresh dill, or ½ teaspoon
  dried dill weed
Salt

Heat the oil in a frying pan that has a tight cover. Place the onions and green peppers in the pan, onions on one side and peppers on the other. Cover and steam over low heat 10 minutes. Add the rest of the ingredients, cover, and cook another 5 minutes.

GREEN PEPPERS STUFFED WITH EGGPLANT

2 large green peppers
1 large eggplant
6 tablespoons olive oil
1 clove garlic, crushed
¼ cup bread crumbs

Cut the green peppers in half lengthwise and remove the seeds. Drop into boiling water for a minute or so, drain, and arrange in a baking pan. Cut the eggplant in small cubes and combine with the garlic and oil. Sauté until lightly browned, about 10 minutes, and fill the pepper shells with the mixture. Sprinkle with the bread crumbs, moisten with a little additional olive oil, and bake in a 375-degree oven 30 minutes.

LEEK SOUFFLÉ

3 large leeks, white part only
4 egg whites
Pinch nutmeg
Salt
2 tablespoons margarine

Cook the sliced leeks in a small amount of water until they are very tender. Drain off the water, add the margarine and seasonings, and mash thoroughly with a potato masher. Fold in the stiffly beaten egg whites, turn into a margarined soufflé dish, and bake 30 minutes in a 350-degree oven.

TINY BOILING ONIONS

Peel 12 or 14 boiling onions and cover them with clam juice. Add 2 tablespoons olive oil, a little thyme, and a bay leaf; simmer very slowly till tender. Remove the onions, strain and reduce the liquid, and salt to taste. Pour back on the onions and reheat. This is a nice accompaniment to fish.

STUFFED ONION SHELLS

3 tablespoons margarine
3 tablespoons flour
2 cups chicken stock
3 very large onions
12 tiny boiling onions
1 tablespoon margarine
⅓ cup bread crumbs

Make a roux of the margarine and flour; gradually stir in the stock to make a thick, creamy sauce. Keep it warm. Boil the large onions in enough salted water to cover for about 25 minutes, or till tender. Drain and cut in half crosswise; remove the centers. Cook the peeled small onions till tender; drain and add to the sauce.

Melt the margarine in a small pan and add the bread crumbs. Now put the big onion halves in a shallow baking dish, and fill the centers with the small onions in the sauce. Sprinkle with the crumbs and slide under the broiler till nicely browned.

SPINACH NESSELRODE

Two 8-ounce bunches fresh spinach
A 2-pound bunch fresh broccoli
Safflower oil mayonnaise

Chop the vegetables as finely as possible. Bring 2 cups water to a boil with 1 teaspoon salt. Add the broccoli and boil 6 minutes; add the spinach and boil 4 minutes. Drain very thoroughly and immediately stir in enough mayonnaise to coat the mixture and hold it together.

RATATOUILLE

¾ pound yellow summer squash
3 large cloves garlic, crushed
6 tablespoons olive oil
1 teaspoon cumin seeds, crushed
½ eggplant
1 teaspoon oregano
3 onions, sliced thin
2 green peppers, seeded and cut into strips
½ teaspoon marjoram
½ teaspoon dill weed
Salt

Peel the eggplant, cut it into small cubes, salt it, and let it stand for a half hour or so. Cube the squash and put it in the bottom of an oiled casserole. To this layer add salt, 1 clove garlic, 2 tablespoons of the oil, and the cumin seeds. Rinse and dry the eggplant, put it in the casserole, and to this layer add salt, another clove of garlic, and the oregano. Now add the onions and green peppers, the rest of the garlic and oil, and the marjoram. Cover and bake in a 350-degree oven 1 hour.

ZUCCHINI

8 zucchini
Salt
Onion salt
Basil

Slice the zucchini on the diagonal, not too thinly. Melt 2 tablespoons margarine and add a garlic clove. When the margarine is hot, remove the garlic; add the zucchini and basil. Cover the pan and shake over high heat until you can hear liquid boiling in the pan. Turn the heat down, add the salt and onion salt, and continue cooking until the zucchini are crisp and firm.

SOUFFLÉ POTATOES

Peel potatoes and slice them about the thickness of a silver dollar. Wipe carefully with paper towels. Use two pans: a deep one with corn oil heated until it throws off a blue smoke and a heavy skillet with just a little margarine melted in it. Put a few potatoes at a time in the skillet and let them just color on both sides. Now remove them with a slotted spoon or spatula and drop them into the hot oil, just one or two at a time; they will puff like balloons. Sprinkle with salt and serve at once.

POTATOES ANNA

6 large potatoes, peeled
¼ pound soft margarine
½ teaspoon salt

Slice the potatoes very thin; soak in cold water; drain and dry. Sprinkle with salt, and line the bottom of a margarined casserole with them. Spread margarine over them, add another layer of potatoes, and keep alternating, ending with a top layer of margarine. Bake in a 450-degree oven about 45 minutes. To serve, invert the casserole on a platter and you should have a brown, molded form.

CANDIED SWEET POTATOES

4 large sweet potatoes, unpeeled
½ cup brown sugar
2 tablespoons margarine
Salt

Boil the potatoes until almost tender; then peel and slice. Place in a shallow baking pan; salt; cover with brown sugar; dot with margarine. Bake in a 350-degree oven about 20 minutes.

COOKING RICE

The Chinese method of cooking rice works very well for me. Simply bring to a boil twice as much water as the amount of rice you use; add salt and the rice; cover and simmer till all the water is absorbed and the rice is tender. I use brown rice because the nutrients haven't been polished away, and find this requires a little more water, since it requires more cooking time.

When serving rice with fish I find that clam juice instead of water is very good, and sometimes I use chicken stock when serving it with chicken. When cooking wild rice I follow the directions on the package, using stock as above, and sometimes adding a few herbs such as thyme or basil. A good handful of chopped parsley with a large dollop of margarine just before serving helps plain rice.

RISOTTO

1 cup rice
1 twist vermicelli, broken in small pieces
1 small onion, chopped
3 cups water or broth

Brown the onion and vermicelli in margarine; add
the rice and the water or broth. Cook over low
heat or bake in a 350-degree oven until all the
water is absorbed.

BIRYANI (Indian-style fried rice)

2 cups long-grain rice, thoroughly washed
½ cup peanut oil
3 onions, peeled and minced
2 cloves garlic, crushed
1 small piece ginger, minced
¼ teaspoon turmeric
Salt

Boil the rice 10 minutes in 4 cups water, drain,
and spread on a flat surface for quick cooling.
Heat the peanut oil very hot; add the onions and
1 cup water. Cook over moderate heat until the
onions are tender and all the water has boiled
away. Stir in the rice, garlic, ginger, and turmeric;
salt to taste. Add about 2 tablespoons margarine
and stir with a wooden spoon until the rice is done
and looks fried.

10

Breads

TRY MAKING your own bread. Admittedly, there are now lots of good breads available that are free of additives and preservatives and are made from all natural ingredients. Again, read that label carefully to be sure you get no milk or eggs!

But the smell of your own bread is worth the whole thing. Suddenly your house is more of a home, and everyone who enters knows it. The yeasty aroma that permeates your kitchen hangs on for days and sharpens appetites immeasurably.

Remember, you should be eating only the basic breads made from yeast, water, and unrefined flour, preferably whole-grain. Our native bread in the United States hardly qualifies as such, but you can eat the native breads of most other countries. The delicious breads of Mexico, France, and Greece come to mind.

Good bread should simply mean something out of the fields with nothing added but a little water and some fire and some skill. I've experimented with combinations of flours and grains such as rye and whole wheat, and come up with some nice Old World bread. Incidentally, my standard morning fare is tea with sprouted-wheat toast (commercial) that is positively dripping in margarine and honey. One of the joys of this diet is that you get thin and stay thin in spite of things like the aforementioned.

Fermented bread—made by mixing flour, water, salt, and yeast—is the easiest to make and the only kind, frankly, I've ever tried. For additional food value you may add malt extract or honey. The object in the kneading of the dough is to incorporate air into it, and it must be kneaded until it's elastic to the touch. When it's covered with a cloth and set aside to rise, it's important to have a warm, draftless place. It so happens that the center of my stove has a grill on it, and apparently the pilot light keeps it just about right. After the bread has risen, which takes from 2 to 4 hours, work it down again and turn it over in the bowl. And when it's risen again and you've worked out the air again and formed it into the loaves, leave them on the board a few minutes to let them rise a little. Be sure your oven is hot enough. As a general rule bread should be baked at high heat to start with, and after it has been thoroughly heated through, the heat is reduced. I always place a pan of water on a rack below the bread; the steam will keep it from burning.

WHOLE-WHEAT BREAD

3 cups warm water
1 cake compressed yeast
2 tablespoons Karo syrup
7 cups whole-wheat flour
1 tablespoon salt

Dissolve the yeast in a little warm water, and mix all the ingredients. Turn out on a lightly floured board and knead at least 10 or 15 minutes. This is hard work, but keep thinking how good the bread's going to be. Then put it into a bowl, cover it with a dishcloth, and set it in a nice warm place to rise. After 2 hours tap it, quite sharply, and if it begins to sink it's ready.

Knead it again, and when it's well worked down return it to the bowl, cover it, and let it rise until it's half again its size. Shape it into loaves, put it into baking pans, and let it rise until it's half again its size. Bake it 1¼ hours, starting at 450 degrees, after 20 minutes reducing to 350, and then again reducing to 300. I like to brush the bread with melted margarine when I take it from the oven. Cool it on a rack.

FRENCH BREAD

2 packages active dry yeast
2 cups warm water
5 cups sifted flour
2 teaspoons salt
½ teaspoon powdered ginger
Corn meal

Add the yeast to the warm water in a large bowl. Stir till well dissolved. Add 2 cups flour, the salt, and the ginger; beat well with a large wooden spoon. Gradually beat in the rest of the flour, until the dough is very stiff. Knead on a floured board 8 to 10 minutes; cover your hands with margarine and pat the dough into a round ball. Place it in a bowl, cover it with a towel, and let it rise in a warm place till in doubles in size. Punch it down to break the rise, and shape into 1 large, long loaf or 2 smaller ones. (I make 2 long, thin, small loaves.) Dust a greased cookie sheet with corn meal, place the loaves on the sheet, and brush the tops with ice water. Cut the tops in slashes diagonally with a scissors, and let the bread rise till doubled again. Place a pan of boiling water in the bottom of the oven. Bake the bread 7 minutes in a preheated 450-degree oven; then reduce the heat to 350 and bake 35 minutes longer. Cool on a rack, after brushing the tops with margarine.

ROGGEBROOD (Dutch Bread)

2½ cups wheat bran
1½ cups rye flour
⅓ cup black molasses
1 teaspoon salt
1½ cups boiling water

Stir everything together, and pack tightly into a 1-pound coffee can. Steam 1¼ hours with the lid on the can in a pan of boiling water (there should be a lid on the pan also). Let the bread cool slightly and invert on a rack. Serve spread with margarine, but be sure to wait till it cools before attempting to slice it.

SOYBEAN BREAD

2 pounds whole-wheat flour
½ pound soybean flour
1 cake compressed yeast
1 pint lukewarm water
½ cup Karo syrup
Salt

Dissolve the yeast in a little warm water and mix all the ingredients into a good thick dough. Let it stand until double its size, in a nice warm place, and then knead it, lapping it over constantly toward the center. Let it rise again to half again its size, and knead it once more. Mold it into loaves, put it in baking pans, and let it rise again until double its size. Bake in a 450-degree oven, watching the browning and turning the heat down as necessary. Cool on a rack.

11

Desserts

DESSERTS ARE somewhat of a problem, since al
most all contain eggs or cream or chocolate o
something else that's *verboten*. However, after
short time on this regime I think you'll find, as
did, that your sweet tooth has dropped out. M
husband and I never have desserts at all whe
we're alone, and these that I do make are mainl
for entertaining. Somehow people expect som
thing at the end of dinner or lunch, and one o
the following recipes will fill the bill nicely.

My husband has his fruit and cheese anywa
but for the most part I think people now woul
rather have a pleasant surprise when they step o.
the scale in the morning.

ANGEL-FOOD CAKE

1 cup egg whites
¼ teaspoon salt
4 tablespoons water
1 teaspoon cream of tartar
1½ cups sugar
1 cup cake flour
1 teaspoon almond extract

Boil the sugar and water together until it forms a thread from the spoon. Beat the egg whites until stiff, gradually beat in the sugar mixture, then add the flavoring, and beat until cooled. Mix and sift the flour and other dry ingredients several times; then gradually fold in the beaten egg-white mixture. Bake in an ungreased angel-food tin at 275 degrees 30 minutes, then at 375 until the cake springs back when pressed with a finger.

MERINGUES WITH CHESTNUT PURÉE

4 egg whites
½ cup fine granulated sugar

Beat the egg whites till foamy; add the sugar gradually and beat until very thick. Drop in 6 rounds from a soupspoon onto oiled aluminum foil about 1 inch apart. Bake at 200 degrees 1 hour. Serve with canned, sweetened chestnut purée.

ALMOND OATMEAL COOKIES

1½ sticks margarine
1 cup brown sugar
¼ cup water
1 generous teaspoon almond flavoring
1 cup flour
½ teaspoon baking soda
1 teaspoon salt
2 cups Quick Quaker Oats
½ cup finely chopped blanched almonds

Mix the margarine, sugar, water, and flavoring and beat till smooth. Sift the dry ingredients together and add to the creamy mixture. Add the Quick Quaker Oats and the almonds. Drop by the teaspoonful onto greased cookie sheets and slightly press down. Bake 14 minutes at 350 degrees.

These cookies are even better when made with a product called Granola instead of the oats.

ALMOND MACAROONS

8-ounce can almond paste
1 cup sugar
2 egg whites

Mix until very smooth. Squeeze through a pastry bag onto foil in half-dollar sizes. Bake at 325 degrees 30 minutes.

ANGEL CREAM

¾ cup grated almonds
5 egg whites
¾ cup sugar
1 teaspoon vanilla

Beat the egg whites till stiff, add ½ cup sugar, and then gently fold in the remaining cup. Add the vanilla and gently fold in the almonds (can be grated in the blender). This should be cold, but since it must be done at the last minute, I keep the ingredients in the refrigerator until ready to make it. It only takes a few minutes to do, and is delicious served in sherbet glasses.

SPICE CAKE WITH CARAMEL FROSTING

1 cup water
⅓ cup margarine
1 cup brown sugar
½ teaspoon cinnamon
½ teaspoon allspice
Good pinch nutmeg
2 cups cake flour
1 teaspoon double-acting baking powder
½ cup chopped almonds and pecans

Boil the water, margarine, sugar, and spices 3 minutes; allow to cool. Sift the flour and baking powder twice and remeasure. Stir gradually into the boiled mixture, and when smooth add the chopped nuts. Bake in a greased tube pan 1 hour

in a preheated 325-degree oven. Make the follow
ing icing:

>2 cups brown sugar
>⅓ cup water
>3 tablespoons margarine
>1 teaspoon vanilla

Stir till dissolved, cover and cook 3 minutes, un
cover and cook without stirring till it forms a bal
in cold water. Add the margarine and let coo
slightly. Add the vanilla and beat till thick and
creamy.

SESAME-SEED COOKIES

>½ cup coconut
>1 cup sesame seeds
>¾ cup corn oil
>1 cup brown sugar
>2 cups flour
>½ teaspoon baking soda
>1 teaspoon baking powder
>½ teaspoon salt
>Vanilla or almond extract, whichever you
> prefer

Spread the coconut and sesame seeds on a baking
sheet and toast them lightly. Cream the oil and
sugar and gradually sift in the dry ingredients
Add the vanilla or almond extract, and mix in the
coconut and seeds. Bake on an oiled cookie shee
about 12 minutes at 350 degrees.

COCONUT SHERBET

1 cup sugar
1 package unflavored gelatin
1 cup water
Two 8-ounce cans coconut juice
2 teaspoons vanilla
1 cup shredded coconut
2 egg whites

Mix ¾ of the sugar with the gelatin in a saucepan, add the water, and stir over low heat till the sugar dissolves. Mix in the coconut juice, vanilla, and coconut and pour into a shallow pan to freeze till solid. Then break up in a bowl and beat till light and fluffy. Whip the egg whites till they form a peak, add the remaining sugar, fold them into the sherbet mixture, and freeze in a covered container. Serve scooped into balls, either passed in a silver bowl or in sherbet glasses.

12

Chinese Cooking

CHINESE COOKING is a delightful change from our daily fare, lends itself beautifully to our diet, of course, and is very quick and easy once you get the hang of it. But first you must get a wok, that conical heavy steel pan. You can get a 14-inch one for about $5.00 either in your local Chinatown or by ordering from the magazine advertisements. Follow the directions concerning its seasoning and with a wooden spoon and spatula you're ready to go.

CHICKEN AND MUSHROOM SOUP

1 chicken breast
1 ounce dried mushrooms
4 cups chicken broth
½ teaspoon salt
1 teaspoon cornstarch
1 ounce bamboo shoots

Slice thinly the chicken and mushrooms. Moisten the cornstarch with a little chicken broth, add the salt, and marinate the chicken. Put the 4 cups broth in the wok, add the mushrooms and bamboo shoots, and bring to a boil; then remove from the heat and add the chicken very carefully—you don't want to lose the cornstarch. Return to the heat, and when the broth has once again reached the boiling point, test to see if the chicken is done. It should be just about right to serve in perhaps 30 seconds' boiling time.

PRAWNS

The wok lends itself admirably to cooking prawns. They may be either shelled beforehand or cooked in their shells and served that way.

PEELED PRAWNS

½ pound prawns, deveined with a small pick poked under the middle of the back (the whole vein should lift out) and shelled
1 tablespoon clam juice
1½ tablespoons soy sauce
2 teaspoons brown sugar
Fingernail-sized piece ginger root
1 scallion, cut in 1-inch pieces
1 teaspoon cornstarch
1 tablespoon safflower or corn oil

Put the oil in the wok and when hot roll it around to coat the sides; add the prawns. Brown quickly on both sides, add the rest of the ingredients except the cornstarch, cover with water, and cook 10 minutes with a lid on. The heat should be just enough to keep the liquid boiling gently. Remove the lid and continue to cook, stirring, until the liquid has been reduced by half. Thicken with the cornstarch, which has been moistened with a little water.

PRAWNS IN THE SHELL

½ pound prawns, deveined but not shelled
1 scallion, chopped
Fingernail-sized piece ginger root
½ clove garlic
1 teaspoon safflower or corn oil
A little wine
1 teaspoon brown sugar

Put the oil in the wok and when hot add the prawns and fry 2 or 3 minutes. Remove the prawns from the wok and put in the scallion, ginger root, and garlic. Put back the prawns, stirring and shaking the wok constantly to allow the seasonings to reach all the shells. Sprinkle with a little wine several times to keep from burning, and add the sugar just as the prawns are done. There should be no liquid left in the wok.

SAUTÉED PRAWNS WITH
BLACK-BEAN SAUCE

- 1 pound prawns, washed, shelled, deveined, and cut into bite-size pieces
- 2 scallions, diced
- 1 slice ginger, minced
- 2 tablespoons black beans
- 2 tablespoons soy sauce
- 4 tablespoons peanut oil (or any vegetable oil)
- 1 teaspoon cornstarch, moistened with a little cold water
- 2 tablespoons water
- 1 teaspoon sugar
- 1 teaspoon salt

Pour a bit of oil in a wok (use an iron skillet if you don't have one) and fry the prawns till they change color. Remove and put on a warm plate. Heat the peanut oil; work in the cornstarch; add the water, ginger, and black beans. Add the seasonings; heat thoroughly; pour the sauce over the prawns. Garnish with the onions.

SHRIMP TOAST

1½ pounds shrimp, deveined and shelled
1 small onion
Pinch ginger
About 12 slices stale French bread
½ teaspoon sugar
1½ teaspoons salt
1 tablespoon cornstarch, moistened with a littl
   cold water
3 tablespoons water
2 cups safflower or corn oil

Chop the shrimp, then the onion; combine all th
ingredients except the oil and spread on the bread
Heat the oil to very hot; deep-fry the bread on th
shrimp side for several minutes; then turn an
brown other side. Drain on paper towels and cu
into small pieces. Serve immediately as an hor
d'oeuvre.

CHINESE OMELET

This recipe could have many variations playec
upon it. I have included it in the Chinese section
because Dr. Dong showed me how to make it, bu

it's perfectly delicious as a breakfast omelet with herbs and parsley for filling, and I experimented once with several crushed cloves of garlic and came up with a great favorite of my husband's.

> 1 4½-ounce can shrimp, or equal amount fresh
> 5 egg whites
> 3 tablespoons chopped Chinese cabbage and/ or bean sprouts
> Safflower oil to cover bottom of frying pan

Sauté the vegetables slowly in the oil, add the shrimp for another minute, and meanwhile break the egg whites into a bowl. Do not beat them! When the vegetables are tender, gently stir them into the egg whites in the bowl. When the mixture is well stirred, drop by the ladleful into the oiled pan, making small omelets about 6 inches across. Use a spatula to keep them from spreading; they will take form almost immediately. Cook them slowly till brown; turn and brown on the other side. Meanwhile put 1 teaspoon cornstarch in a bowl with a little cold water; add some soy sauce and a pinch of sugar; mix well. After the omelets are removed from the pan, pour this mixture into it, and stir carefully till it becomes a clear, glaze-like sauce to serve over the omelets.

SHRIMP WITH VEGETABLES

2 tablespoons corn oil
1 pound medium-sized raw shrimp, deveined
and shelled
1 tablespoon soy sauce
1 clove garlic, crushed
½ teaspoon minced fresh ginger
4 stalks celery, thinly sliced
1 onion, thinly sliced
6-ounce can water chestnuts, thinly sliced
4 cups fresh bean sprouts
2 tablespoons cornstarch, moistened with a
little cold water
½ teaspoon salt
2 tablespoons soy sauce
¾ cup chicken broth

Heat the wok and put in 1 tablespoon of the oil. When very hot put in the shrimp, soy sauce, garlic, and ginger. Stir 2 or 3 minutes until the shrimp turns nicely pink. Turn out onto the serving dish. Mix the cornstarch, salt, soy sauce, and chicken broth. Reheat the wok, add the remaining oil, add the vegetables and the cornstarch mixture, and simmer till the vegetables are done crisply. It will only take a few minutes. Pour everything over the shrimp and serve.

SHRIMP AND CHICKEN WITH EGGPLANT

2 chicken breasts
½ cup corn oil
1 large clove garlic, crushed
1 teaspoon grated fresh ginger
1 small eggplant, unpeeled
½ pound small shrimp
2 tablespoons cornstarch, moistened with a
    little cold water
2 tablespoons soy sauce
6-ounce can water chestnuts, sliced thickly
3 tablespoons chicken broth
Chopped parsley

Cut the eggplant into sticks about the size of your
little finger. Cover them with boiling water, cover
the bowl, and let stand about 10 minutes. Drain
well. Skin and bone the chicken breasts, slice the
meat into pieces the same size as the eggplant
sticks, and mix with the cornstarch and soy sauce.
Heat the wok; add the oil and then the garlic,
ginger, and eggplant. Stir and toss until the eggplant is brown; then add the chicken mixture,
shrimp, and chestnuts. Cook in the same manner
until the chicken is done—it will only take a very
few minutes. Add the broth, cook another minute,
and serve sprinkled with the parsley. If desired,
additional soy sauce may be served.

SHRIMP WITH WALNUTS

2 pounds shrimp, shelled and cleaned
3 cups water, salted
½ pound walnut halves
2 tablespoons cornstarch
3 tablespoons soy sauce
1 green pepper, cut in strips

Boil the shrimp in the salted water 5 minutes; drain and save the liquid. Put the walnuts in a 450-degree oven 4 or 5 minutes; then rub off their brown outer skins. Mix the cornstarch with 1½ cups of the shrimp water; add the shrimp, soy sauce, and green pepper. Cook 3 minutes and add the nuts.

SHRIMP AND GREEN PEAS

2 pounds shrimp, deveined and shelled
1½ cups peas
½ teaspoon powdered ginger
1 teaspoon sugar
1 teaspoon salt
1 teaspoon soy sauce
1 teaspoon cornstarch
3 tablespoons cold water
2 cloves garlic, minced or crushed
3 tablespoons peanut oil
3 scallions, chopped

Heat the oil in your wok, add the shrimp, and brown briskly. Remove the shrimp; add the scallions, ginger, garlic, and peas. Combine the cornstarch, salt, sugar, and soy sauce in a smooth paste, thinning with the water, and add this mixture to the vegetables in the wok. Cook just till the peas are done, about 3 or 4 minutes at most, and add the shrimp. When everything is hot, serve immediately.

SHRIMP BALLS

2 pounds shrimp, deveined and shelled
18 water chestnuts
1 tablespoon cornstarch, moistened with a little cold water
2 teaspoons salt
½ teaspoon sesame oil
1 egg white
2 cups vegetable oil

Chop the shrimp very fine; chop the water chestnuts. Combine all the ingredients except the egg white and the vegetable oil. Heat this oil; form the shrimp-chestnut mixture into balls, dip them in egg white, and drop them into the oil. The balls will float when done, but fry till they are golden brown.

CANTONESE SOFT FRIED CHOW MEIN

1 pound egg-free noodles (cellophane or pea starch, for instance)
3 tablespoons vegetable oil
1 tablespoon cornstarch, moistened with a little cold water
3 tablespoons soy sauce
½ teaspoon sugar
½ teaspoon sesame oil
1 teaspoon salt
1 clove garlic, minced
1 thin slice ginger
½ pound crab, lobster, or shrimp
½ cup shredded or chopped bamboo shoots
½ cup bean sprouts, dried ends cut off
½ cup shredded or chopped celery
1 cup shredded or chopped Chinese cabbage
¼ cup thinly sliced water chestnuts
2 ounces Chinese mushrooms, soaked in cold water about 15 minutes, rinsed and cut up
6 snow peas, cut diagonally into ½-inch pieces
2 scallions, minced

Cook the noodles till almost done. Drain, rinse with cold water, and divide into two batches. Put 1 tablespoon oil in the wok and when hot fry half the noodles till slightly crisp; then fry the other half. Remove and place on a large serving dish.

Have ready beside the wok: the cornstarch and water mixed with the soy sauce, sugar, and sesame oil; all the vegetables, the seasonings, and the seafood.

Heat the wok over a high flame; add the remaining 2 tablespoons oil and the salt, garlic, and ginger. Add the seafood and stir for a few minutes; then add the bamboo shoots, bean sprouts, and celery, cabbage, water chestnuts, and mushrooms. Add 1 cup water; cover and cook 3 minutes. Uncover and stir 30 seconds. Next add the snow peas and thicken with the cornstarch mixture. Stir in the scallions; then add more sesame oil (after tasting to see if the flavor of sesame appeals to you). Remove from the flame, pour everything over the noodles, and garnish with Chinese parsley.

KOREAN BEAN SPROUTS

4 cups bean sprouts
2 scallions
2 tablespoons soy sauce
2 tablespoons roasted sesame seeds
2 teaspoons safflower or corn oil
Salt

Wash fresh young bean sprouts in cold water, snipping off any dried-up ends. Cover with boiling water and cook 3 minutes; drain. Cut the tops off the scallions, slice them into 1-inch lengths, and set aside. Chop the white part of the scallions and add to the bean sprouts; also add the soy sauce, sesame seeds, and oil. Cook 2 or 3 minutes; then add the sliced scallion tops. Cook 1 or 2 minutes, stirring frequently; add salt and serve as you would any vegetable.

BASS WITH BEAN SPROUTS

3-4 pieces sea bass
¼ cup chopped scallions
4 tablespoons soy sauce
1 tablespoon slivered fresh ginger
5 tablespoons peanut oil
1 cup water
1 pound bean sprouts

Put 3 tablespoons oil in the wok; when heated roll around to coat the wok and add the fish, the onions, 3 tablespoons soy sauce, the ginger, and the water. Cover the wok tightly, bring to a rapid boil, and allow to simmer about 45 minutes, or until the fish flakes easily. In the meantime, cook the bean sprouts in 2 tablespoons oil and 1 tablespoon soy sauce 5 minutes, put on a large platter, top with the steamed fish, and over this pour the remaining juices. Serve with rice and Chinese peas.

CHINESE-STYLE LOBSTER

3 one-pound lobsters
2 tablespoons soy sauce
1 small onion, chopped fine
2 tablespoons water

Split the lobsters lengthwise and clean well (I have this done at the fish market). Place them on a rack either in a steamer or in your wok with a tight lid, with boiling water below. Mix the soy sauce, onion, and water and distribute on the lobsters; cover tightly and steam 10 minutes. I almost prefer this to any other way of doing lobster, since it never gets tough. If you like, you can serve melted margarine, in addition, in a little pot beside each lobster half.

Since the Chinese don't go in for desserts, you might serve candied coconut, preserved ginger, dried litchi nuts, salted almonds, or cashews at the end of your Chinese dinner.

WOK-FRIED OYSTERS

    2 tablespoons corn oil
    1 jar oysters (about 10 ounces)
    2 teaspoons soy sauce

Pour the jar of oysters into a pan of simmering water and cook 4 minutes. Drain. Heat the wok, add the oil, and when very hot add the oysters and soy sauce. Cook until the oysters' edges start to curl and they are done, about 3 minutes.

BEAN CURD AND SPINACH

Bean curd is made from our old friend the soybean. It's known as the "Wonderful Bean" in China, undoubtedly for the same reason that we treasure it. The curd is actually the moisture, or milk, from the soybean. There are different textures—some soft, some hard. I suggest you experiment a little when buying it.

    16 pieces bean curd, about 2 × 1 × 1 inches
    ½ pound spinach cut in 2-inch pieces
    1 teaspoon cornstarch
    1 clove garlic
    1 tablespoon soy sauce
    ½ teaspoon salt
    1 teaspoon brown sugar
    4 tablespoons safflower or corn oil

Cover the bean curd with water to which the salt has been added; soak 10 minutes; drain. Place 1 tablespoon oil in a flat pan and brown the bean curd carefully. You will find you can turn it over with the side of a knife. Add the soy sauce, sugar, and a little water; simmer 5 to 10 minutes. Now put 3 tablespoons oil in your wok and when hot toss in the spinach, garlic, and a little more salt.

Stir and toss till almost done; add the bean curd
and allow to cook without stirring 1 or 2 minutes.
Thicken with the cornstarch (moistened with
water) and serve. A few drops of sesame oil may
be added if you like.

CREAMED CORN SOUP WITH CRAB

16-ounce can creamed corn
½ cup crab meat
2 tablespoons cornstarch, moistened with a
   little cold water
Small bit thinly sliced ginger or pinch
   powdered ginger
2 tablespoons vegetable oil
¼ teaspoon salt
1 teaspoon sherry (this little bit can't hurt you)
4 cups water
2 egg whites, slightly whipped

To the water add the ginger, sherry, oil, and salt;
bring to a boil. Add the remaining ingredients,
folding the egg whites in last. Serve very hot in
Chinese bowls with china spoons.

13

Hawaiian Cooking

WE HAVE BEEN fortunate enough to live on the beautiful islands of Hawaii twice, and have made innumerable visits. I always feel marvelous when I am there, and perhaps the abundance of fish accompanied by plain vegetables has something to do with it. The native cuisine is simplicity itself, but served with such charm! Naturally, not all the ingredients mentioned in the following recipes are available everywhere, but I believe one could find some of them most anyplace. *Poi*, for instance, is available in cans—it tastes terrible, but it's the *idea*, you know! The basic things are fresh ginger, garlic and onion, soy sauce, *pa'a kai*—which is the rock salt used for cooking (the white kind) and for the table (the red kind)—and raw sugar (the unrefined sugar milled in Hawaii).

Pupus is the Hawaiian name for appetizers, and includes myriads of tasty little things which could be made into a buffet supper. I have a very small hibachi, the Japanese charcoal grill, which I use on the hearth so that the fumes go up the chimney; scallops dipped in soy sauce and oil and grilled are good this way. A cold lobster cut up in convenient pieces with a bowl of safflower oil mayonnaise nearby is easy and nice. A huge tray of carrots, celery, cauliflower, and green pepper is good with the following dip: 1 cup safflower oil mayonnaise; finely chopped onion, including green; can shrimp, lobster, or crab, shredded; garlic salt and soy sauce.

The Hawaiian fish names won't help you much in New York or Kansas City, but *amaama, a'u, kawakawa, epelu,* and *ulua* turn out to be bonita, mullet, marlin, mackerel, and pompano. These can be either fillets or steaks, cooked in any of several typical ways. They might be marinated first in soy sauce and garlic with a thin slice of ginger, then brushed with margarine and broiled. Or they might be steamed in a dish over boiling water and then rubbed with peanut oil and soy sauce. Or sautéed quickly, after being marinated, till very crisp and brown. And, most colorfully, they might be baked in *ti* leaves with a slice of onion. Be sure to wrap the leaves securely, tying the ends with string if necessary, and bake them in a roasting pan with a little water.

ABALONE

Cut 1 pound canned abalone into bite-sized pieces. Serve very cold in a bowl with a little of the liquid and on the side toothpicks and soy sauce.

SASHIMI

This is normally served raw. I steam it for a very short time instead, and chill it well. It should be fresh albacore or some other firm, delicate white fish. Remove the skin, and with a very sharp knife cut the fish diagonally in very thin slices, overlapping as you go so that you can pick up the slices all together and lay them on a bed of shredded lettuce. Serve very cold with soy sauce.

SHRIMP TEMPURA

Prepare 2 pounds raw shrimp, leaving the tail on for a handle. Dip in ½ cup flour mixed with ½ cup cornstarch, salt, and 1 cup clam juice. Fry in deep, hot corn oil.

MAHIMAHI

The *mahimahi* is the best of the Hawaiian fish. It's expensive and hard to get, but the firm white meat is absolutely wonderful. I must mention here that I caught a 50-pound mahimahi off Oahu recently, and as I was struggling to bring him in, the thought occurred to me that there was something eminently suitable about the rehabilitated arthritic bringing in the source of her cure, so to speak. Alas, there was no one around with a camera or there would be a picture of that fish and me right here.

Well, back to cooking. Grill the mahimahi fillets

in a wire grill that holds the fish securely on both sides. Baste with melted margarine and grill about 5 minutes on each side.

The Outrigger Club on Waikiki has been famous for its mahimahi for many years. Unfortunately its recipe calls for milk, eggs, and cognac, but the following will do nicely as a substitute.

Slice the mahimahi very thin, about ½ inch. Marinate in soy sauce and onion slices about 10 minutes; then dust with flour. Sauté in a mixture of half oil and half margarine until golden brown. Place the fish on a warm serving platter. Discard the remaining oil in the pan; in the same pan melt plenty of fresh margarine. Sizzle until brown, add sliced almonds and chopped parsley, and pour this over the fish. The Outrigger Club garnishes it with a bouquet of parsley and a vanda orchid.

LOMI SALMON

Take a 1-pound piece of salt salmon and soak 3 hours, changing the water from time to time. Shred the salmon and mix with finely chopped scallions and serve very cold with *poi*. You can make do with canned salmon.

COCONUT CHICKEN

Rub chicken breasts with oil and dip them in French bread crumbs mixed with an equal amount of grated coconut. You may add just a pinch of curry powder, since I consider this dish a special treat. Place the breasts in a shallow baking pan and dribble over them 1 stick melted margarine; bake about 50 minutes. Serve with taro cakes and spinach with coconut milk.

· TARO CAKES

Where you get the taro root is your problem, but once you have it, boil it till it's very tender; then mash it while still hot, adding meanwhile a little water, 1 teaspoon baking powder, 1 teaspoon sugar, and 1 stick margarine. Wet your hands and form the taro into small cakes; place them on a greased pan; make a dent for more margarine in each; and bake at 350 degrees 20 minutes.

COCONUT SPINACH

Cook three 12-ounce packages frozen chopped spinach and drain very well. Add 1 cup coconut milk (this is available canned) and salt to taste. Reheat before serving.

PARSLEY TEMPURA

Mix ½ cup flour, ½ cup cornstarch, ½ teaspoon baking powder, ½ teaspoon salt, and 1 cup water; beat smooth. Dip large fresh parsley sprigs in this mixture and fry quickly in deep, hot corn oil.

SAUTÉED CABBAGE

Remove the core of a tender young head of cabbage. Cut in small squares and sauté over high heat in lots of margarine for just about a minute. It will be just tender crisp. Add salt, a little dill weed, and a tablespoon or so of safflower oil mayonnaise.

MACADAMIA NUT DESSERT

¾ cup sugar
1¼ cups light corn syrup
½ cup melted margarine
4 egg whites, beaten
1 teaspoon vanilla
1½ cups diced macadamia nuts
Coconut cream (canned)

Beat the sugar, corn syrup, margarine, and vanilla together; add the beaten egg whites and nuts and turn into a margarined 8-inch-square baking pan. Bake in a 375-degree oven 35 to 40 minutes. Cool on a rack, spoon into dessert dishes, and serve topped with the coconut cream.

14

Entertaining

WHEN I FIRST STARTED this way of eating I cooked separately for myself; for about the first month I broiled steak or lamb chops for my husband and fish for myself. Gradually my kind of food became his kind of food—I'm not sure he even noticed the change! However, with our friends I took it a little slower; I adjusted to their world. Now, after almost three years, I'm glad to announce I've got them adjusted to *my* world! It's so much easier that way!

In the first place, I don't think people ever really notice what the ingredients are if a meal is flavorful and attractively presented. I always serve a soup, and it's always something a little different from anything they get elsewhere. I like a green salad next, California style, and then the entree can be anything from a whole salmon, decorated on a plank surrounded by little new potatoes and vegetables, to a delectable dish of chicken breasts with a wine sauce. I've had great success with my Angel Cream for dessert, incidentally.

The Chinese menu is sure-fire—guests don't realize at all that it's a special diet. The decor is important: Go out and furnish yourself with good Chinese mats, lacquer bowls and chopsticks, teacups—the works. You can serve warm rice wine to the others if you like, and I think fortune cookies are available in many places to pass around for dessert. You can make an amusing party out of the Hawaiian recipes—add a few *ti* leaves or a reasonable facsimile to decorate the table; use your imagination with some tropical flowers. It's an easy charmer. You might serve the salad in a giant clamshell if you have one; large wooden bowls might hold the shrimp, with smaller ones for sauces or nuts. Surround these with lots of ferns and tuberous begonias. Light it with hurricane lamps, and you have a tropical setting.

Living in California, and particularly living as we do on a beautiful lagoon, lends itself to outdoor entertaining. I find I can do a complete barbecue party by serving tunaburgers, French rolls, coleslaw, potato salad, baked beans, corn on the cob, and a platter of attractively arranged raw vegetables.

One thing—your friends won't exactly hate you for giving them your kind of food. Most people these days are watching their weight, and if they leave your table with a pound lost they'll love you; they'll be happy anyway if they just hold their own!

15

Restaurants

FOLLOWING THIS somewhat proscribed regime in your own kitchen is one thing; circulating, as we all must do to a certain extent, in the outside world is another. When you accept an invitation from friends for luncheon or dinner, make up your mind in advance you'll probably come away hungry—unless, of course, they happen to be the kind of friends who know about your diet in advance and cooperate. Restaurants, on the other hand, present a different picture because here you have a chance to dictate your wishes. Almost all menus will offer something you can eat, particularly after you become aware enough to demand that your fish be sautéed in margarine and oil, and nothing else, that your vegetables be served plain. I've found our good restaurants to be most adaptable and cooperative, and have found some to have some splendid recipes that are completely acceptable.

LAZIO'S SALMON EN BROCHETTE

Eureka, far up on the rugged northernmost coast of California, boasts an unequaled seafood restaurant called Lazio's. One dines in a unique atmosphere right on the processing-plant wharf with the fishing boats just outside the windows, their nets still dripping. The freshness of the fish undoubtedly is a factor in the quality of the cuisine, but I think this simple method of preparing salmon could be duplicated in your own kitchen.

> Chunks of fresh salmon, 1½ to 2 inches square
> Small white onions, parboiled
> Chunks of green pepper, parboiled
> Fresh mushrooms, lightly oiled

Thread the fish and vegetables alternately on long skewers and slide the skewers under the broiler. Broil, turning frequently, until the fish is easily flaked with a fork. Serve on a bed of rice to which you've added plenty of margarine.

FILET OF REX SOLE BARDELLI

This recipe comes from Bardelli's, one of San Francisco's oldest restaurants, which is filled with the city's special ambiance.

Roll the fillets in flour and deposit them in a hot skillet with margarine; add sliced scallion tops, sliced mushrooms, crab legs, and shrimp. Season with salt. Turn the fish over once, add one wine glass of sauterne (or substitute clam juice) and a little chopped parsley. Serve on a hot platter.

Cooking this dish will take less than 10 minutes.

ESCABECHE

Caprice, in Tiburon, California, hangs over the water looking across to a sensational view of San Francisco. It's small and intimate, with the charming owner and his wife always on hand to oversee the splendid cuisine.

The cold, vinegar-piquant fish in the following recipe can be an hors d'oeuvre, a first course, or a rather remarkable main course when you accompany them with hot potatoes baked with peels on and red wine.

Make Escabeche at least two days before eating. Even longer is better. You can keep it in the refrigerator for at least a week, and it gets better and better.

The Portuguese often use their very small, mild fish, *carapau* (saurel), or sardines for Escabeche. Sometimes they use slices of larger fish.

2 pounds steaks or fillets of mild, firm, white-
fleshed fish (such as sea bass, rockfish, halibut) about ½ inch thick
Salt
Salad oil (no olive)
2 large sweet onions, very thinly sliced
¾ cup olive oil
2 carrots, peeled and grated
1 cup clam juice
2 large cloves garlic, minced or mashed
2 bay leaves, broken
About 2 teaspoons salt
1 teaspoon paprika

Season the fish lightly with salt; let stand 15 minutes. Quickly fry in a generous amount of salad
oil until the flesh loses translucency and flakes
easily with a fork. Allow to cool; remove any skin
and bones; break into large chunks. In a large frying pan, sauté the onions in olive oil until limp.
Stir in the carrots, clam juice, garlic, bay leaves,
salt, paprika. Allow to cool. Arrange the fish and
the onion mixture in alternate layers in a deep
earthenware jar or bowl or glass jar. Cover and
chill at least 2 days. Makes about 10 first-course
servings or 6 supper servings.

ARROZ CON POLLO

This comes from El Borro, a charming little Mexican restaurant on Tiburon's main street.

    ½ cup olive oil
    1 frying chicken cut into serving pieces
    1 small onion, chopped
    1 clove garlic, minced
    ⅛ teaspoon saffron
    2½ cups chicken broth
    Salt
    1 cup uncooked rice
    ¼ pound mushrooms, sliced
    4 artichoke hearts
    A few sliced pimentos

Heat the oil; brown the chicken on both sides. Add the onion and garlic; fry a few minutes; then add the saffron, dissolved in chicken broth; salt. Cover and cook 20 minutes. Add the rice; stir well; cover again and simmer 30 minutes longer or until all the liquid has been absorbed and the chicken is tender. Add the artichoke hearts and pimentos for the last 10 minutes of cooking.

ABALONE DORÉ AMANDINE

Nick's Fish Market is a restaurant specializing in seafood, halfway between Diamond Head and Waikiki. Both the food and service are superb.

To make its recipe for Abalone Doré Amandine, use 5-6 abalone per person. Pound the fish and dip in flour mixed with salt. Then dip in beaten egg whites and fry in hot peanut oil, 1½ minutes on each side. Take the abalone out of the oil and dry with a paper cloth. Melt margarine in a skillet; when it starts to turn brown, add sliced almonds. Pour this over the abalone and serve with parsley.

RED SNAPPER—BELLE ALLIANCE

Here is another recipe from Nick's Fish Market.

    Sliced onions
    Sliced green pepper
    Sliced fresh mushrooms
    Sliced pimentos
    Dash white wine
    Chicken stock
    Tabasco
    Garlic
    Margarine

Sauté the above items. Bake the snapper 10 minutes at 425 degrees. Pour the sautéed items over the fish and serve with boiled Irish potatoes.

LARK CREEK CHICKEN-VEGETABLE SOUP

The Lark Creek Inn is in an old, remodeled Victorian house. The dining room is glass-roofed to show off the splendid trees. It's a great place for a country-style evening.

2 quarts chicken stock
2 cups diced chicken breasts
1 teaspoon salt
½ cup diced celery
2 scallions, chopped
1 carrot, sliced
1 medium-sized onion, sliced
3 whole cloves
½ teaspoon nutmeg
1 tablespoon chopped parsley
1 bay leaf (fresh, if possible)
2 cups mixed vegetables of your choice (Lark Creek uses zucchini, mushrooms, green beans)
1 cup cooked rice

Add the diced chicken and the salt to the stock and bring to a boil. Skim the surface until no more fat rises. Allow to simmer 1 hour. Add the remaining ingredients. Bring to a boil and skim again. Simmer 2 hours. Serves 12.

Index

191

ABOUT THE AUTHORS

DR. COLLIN H. DONG, who has practiced medicine for over forty years, is a graduate of Stanford Medical School, a member of the American Medical Association, the California Medical Association and the San Francisco Medical Society and a staff member of the Chinese Hospital in San Francisco. He is an art collector, as well as an artist in his own right. Dr. Dong and his wife have three children.

JANE BANKS, who is the wife of a retired Marine brigadier general and the mother of a married daughter, lives in Belvedere, California. Besides being a peerless cook and hostess, she is a talented painter and professional decorator. Weekends find her canoeing, swimming, bicycling and hiking with her husband, sometimes all on the same day.

How's Your Health?